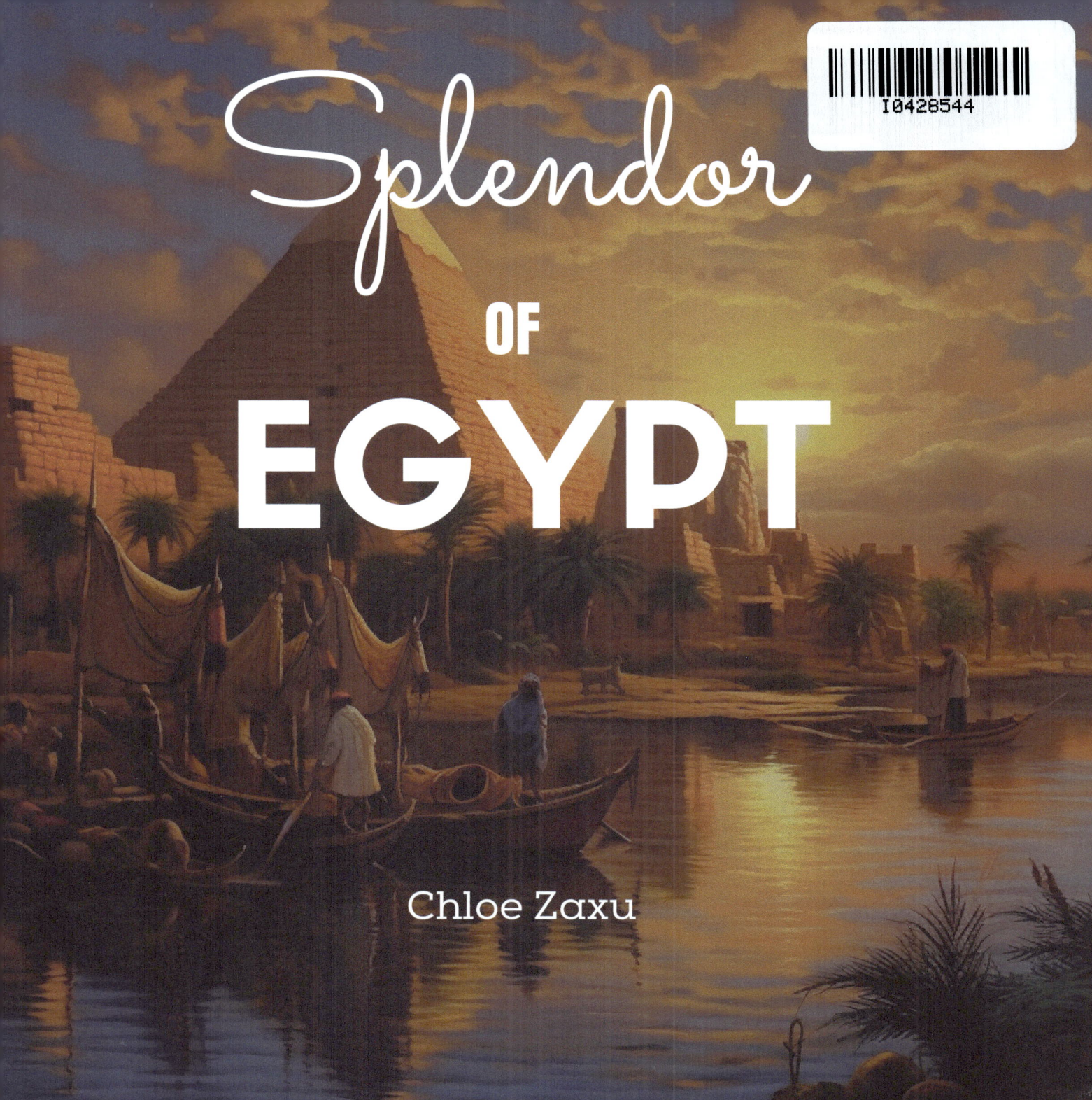

Splendor

OF

EGYPT

Chloe Zaxu

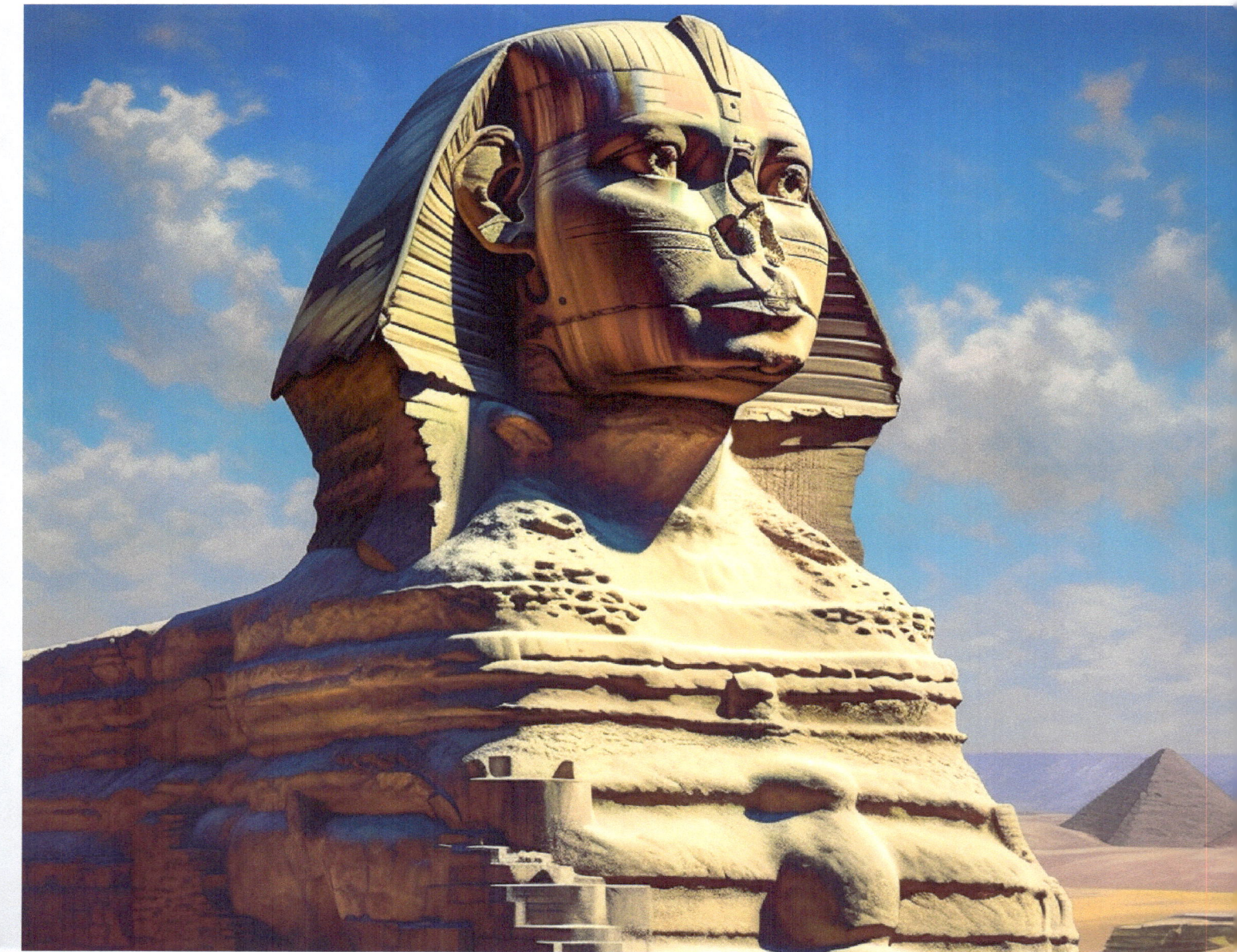

SPHINX

The mysterious statue that guards the Giza plateau.

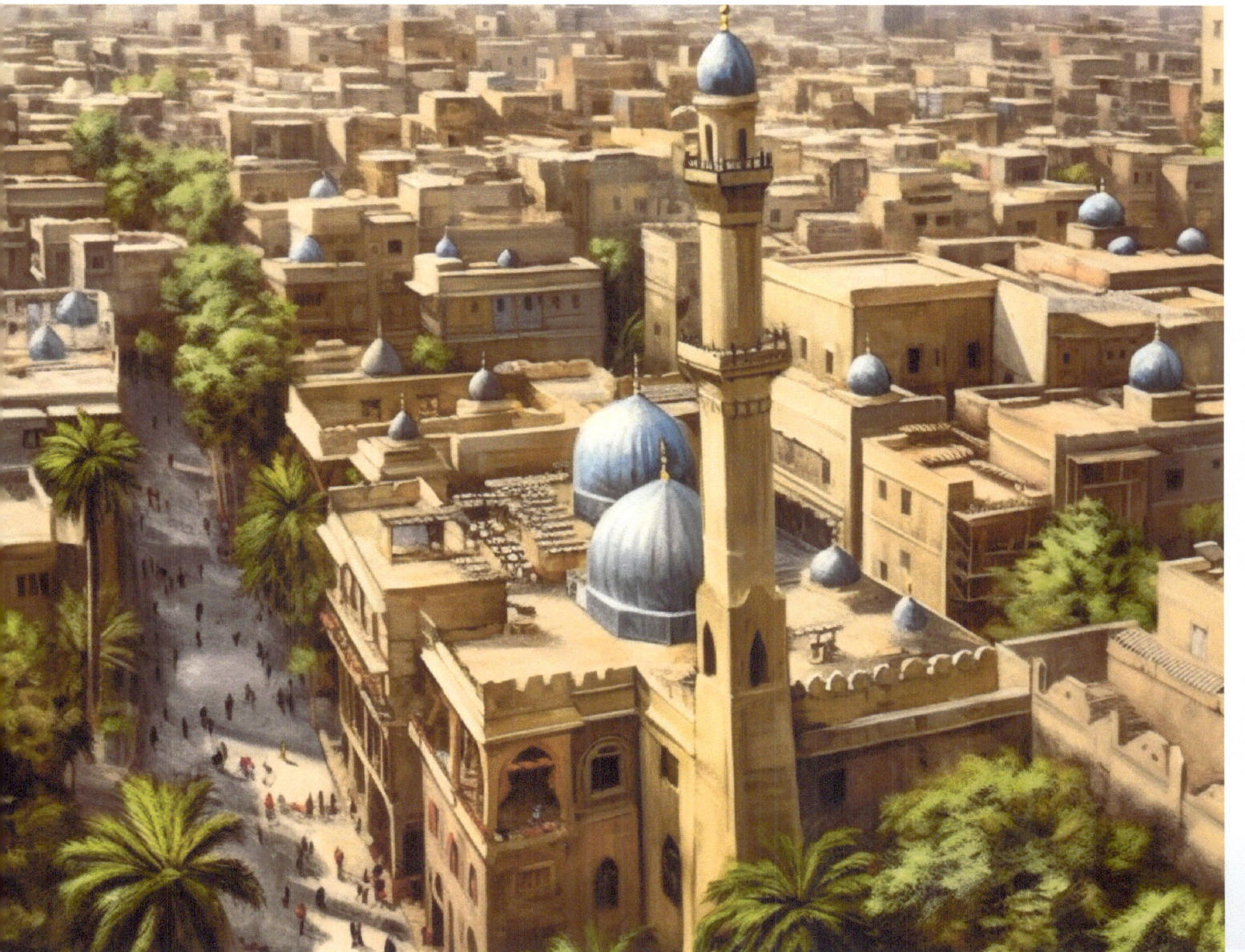

COPTIC CAIRO

A part of Old Cairo which encompasses the Babylon Fortress.

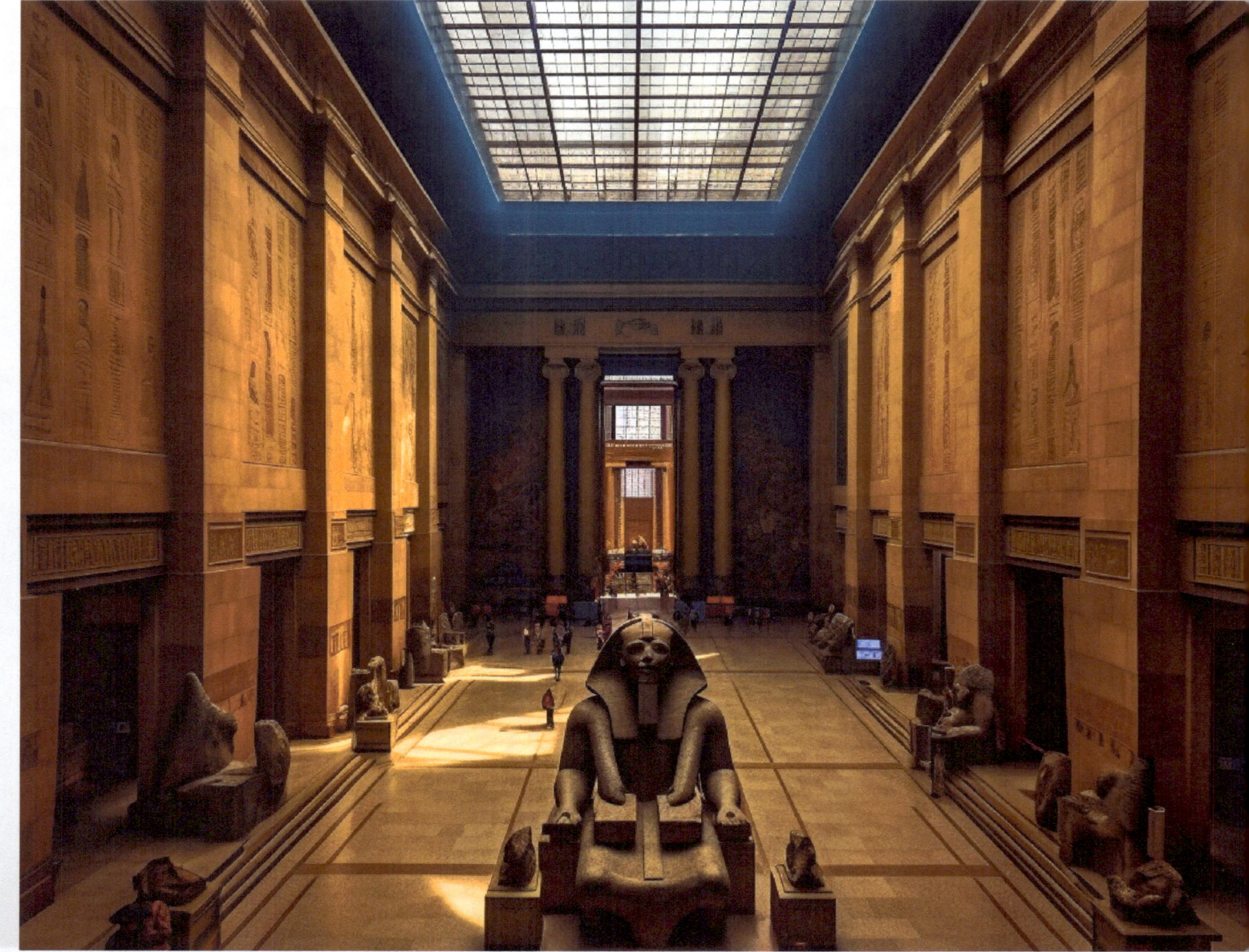

CAIRO EGYPTIAN MUSEUM

A place to see Egypt's ancient artifacts, including
Tutankhamun's treasures.

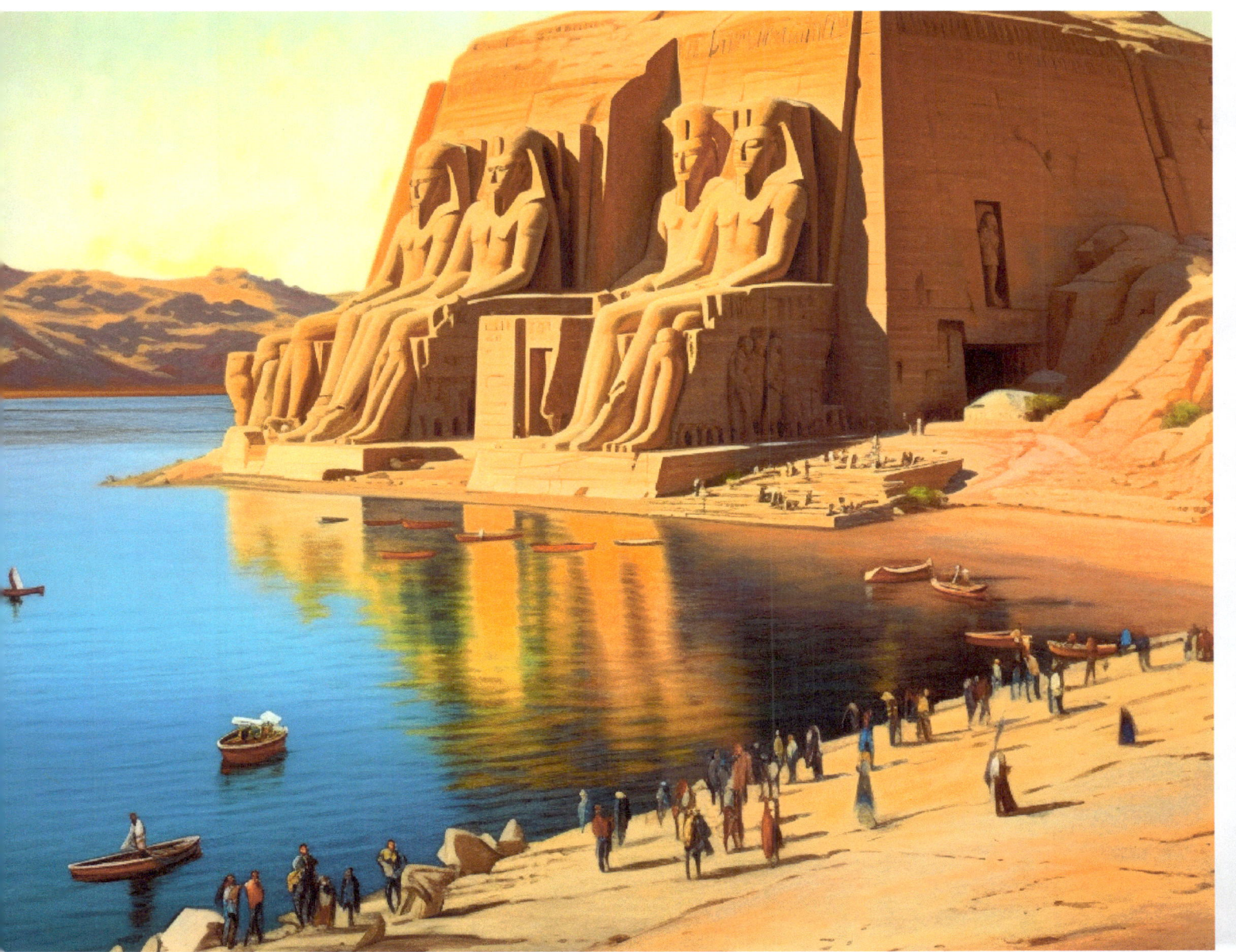

ABU SIMBEL

Two massive rock temples in Nubia

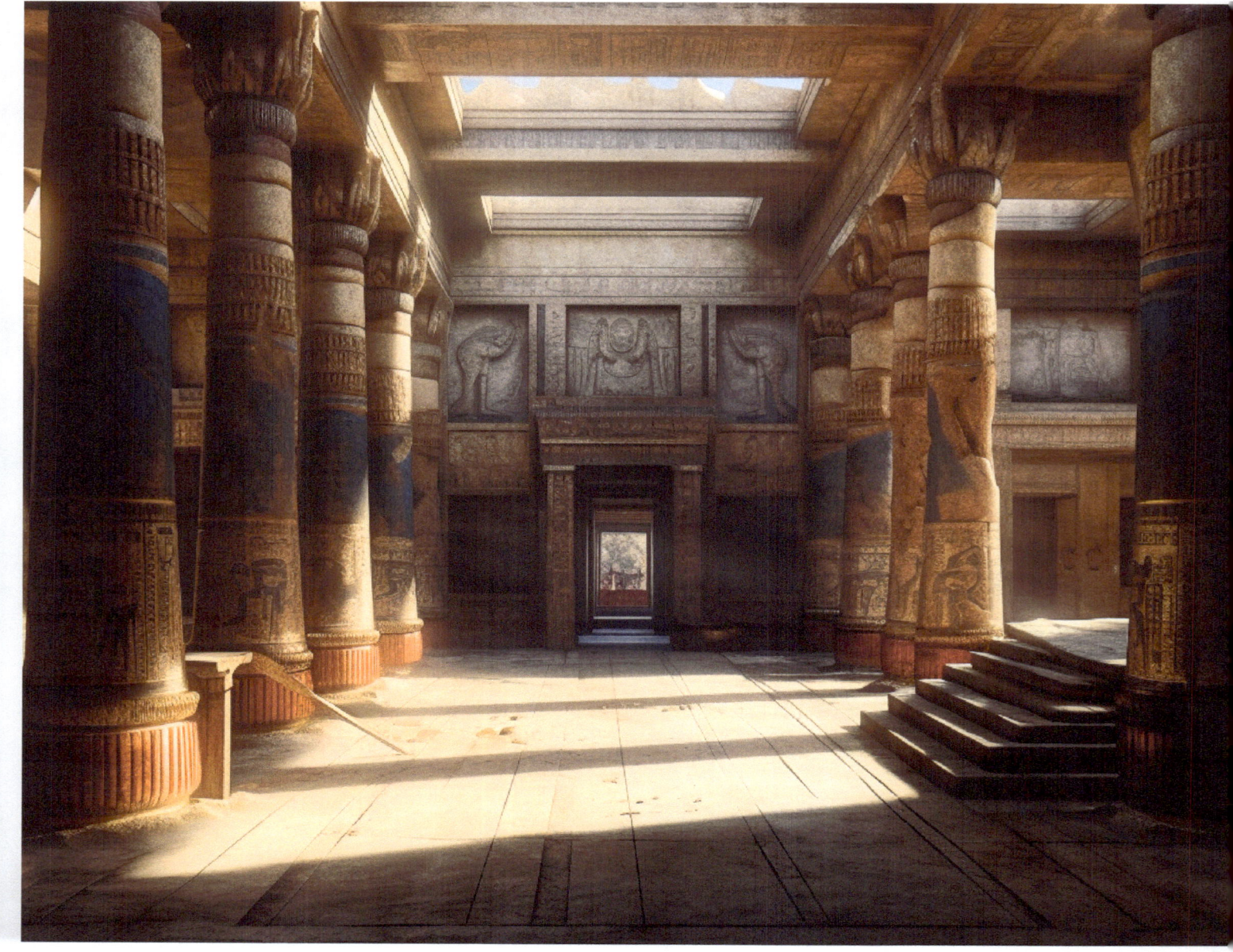

ABYDOS TEMPLE

One of the most important religious sites of Ancient Egypt.

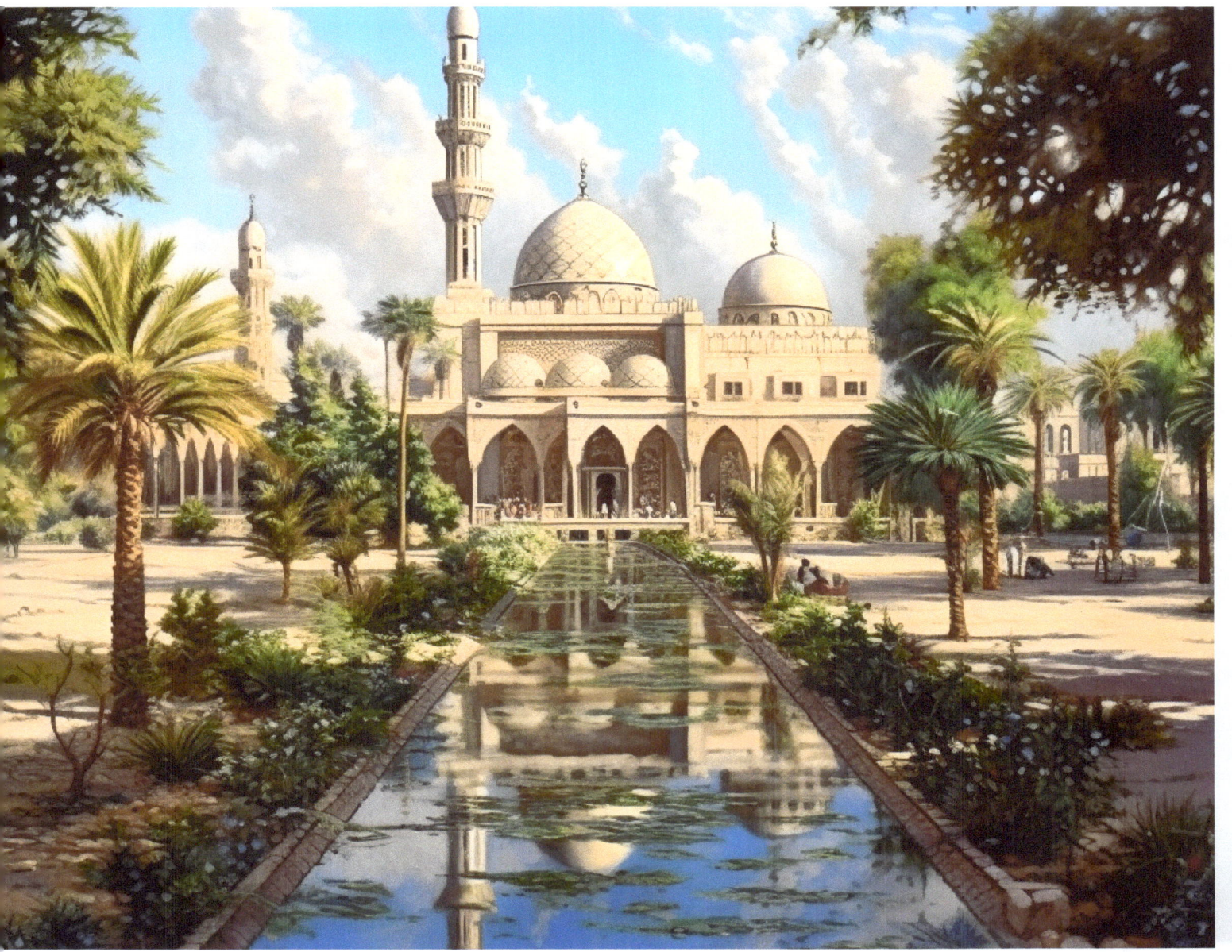

AL-AZHAR PARK

A beautifully landscaped park in Cairo.

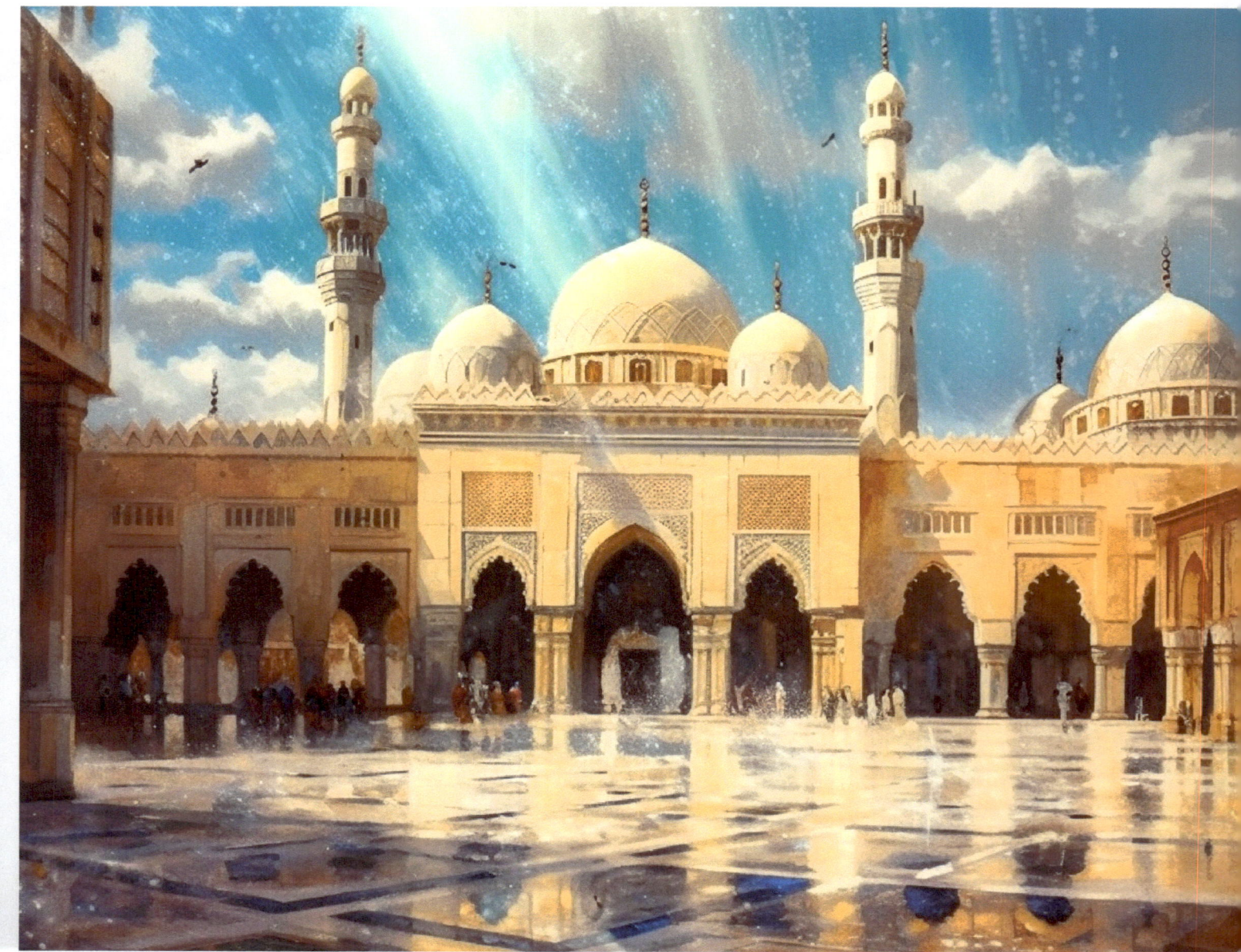

AL-AZHAR MOSQUE

An influential mosque and university in Cairo.

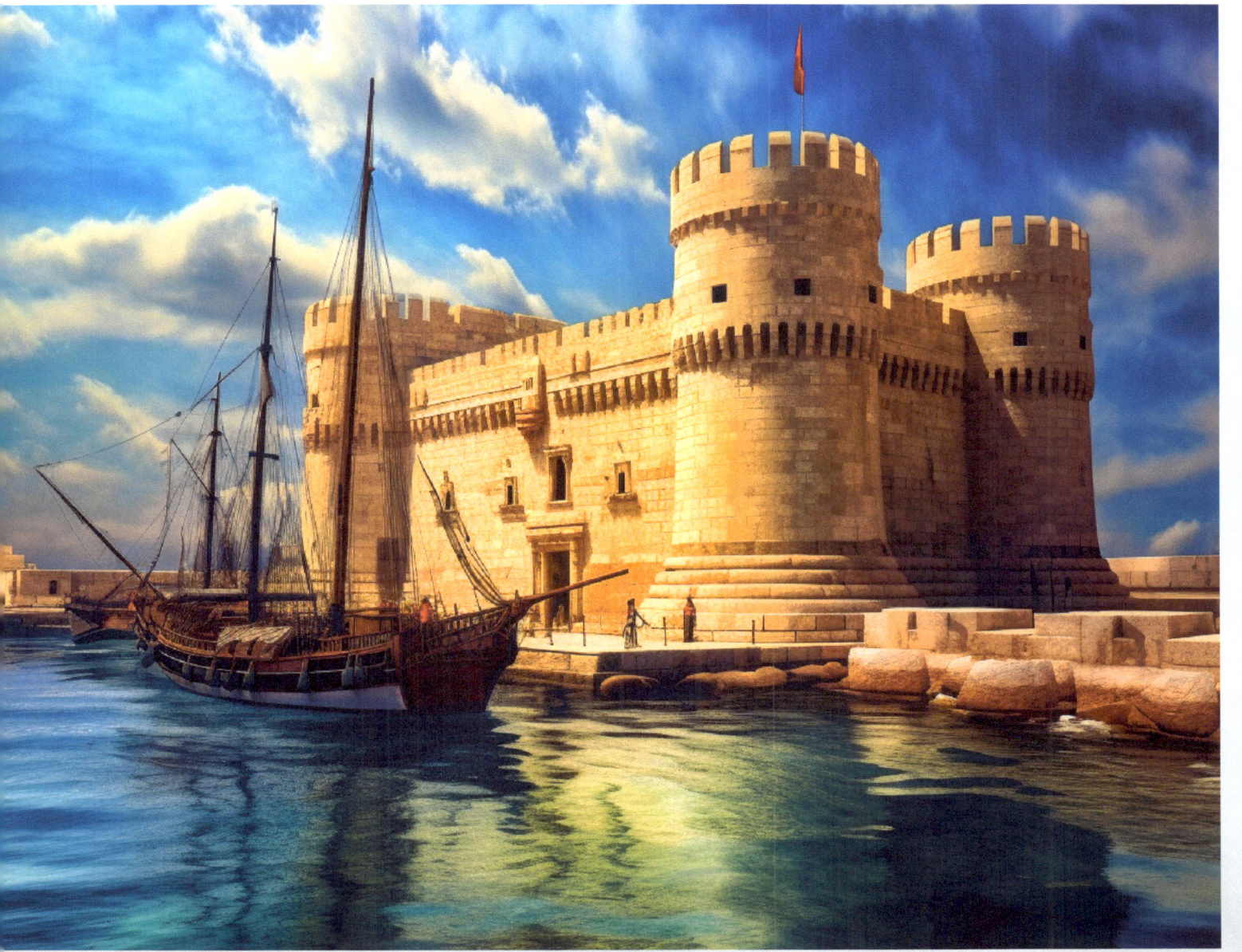

ALEXANDRIAS QAITBAY CITADEL

A 15th-century fortress on the Mediterranean Sea.

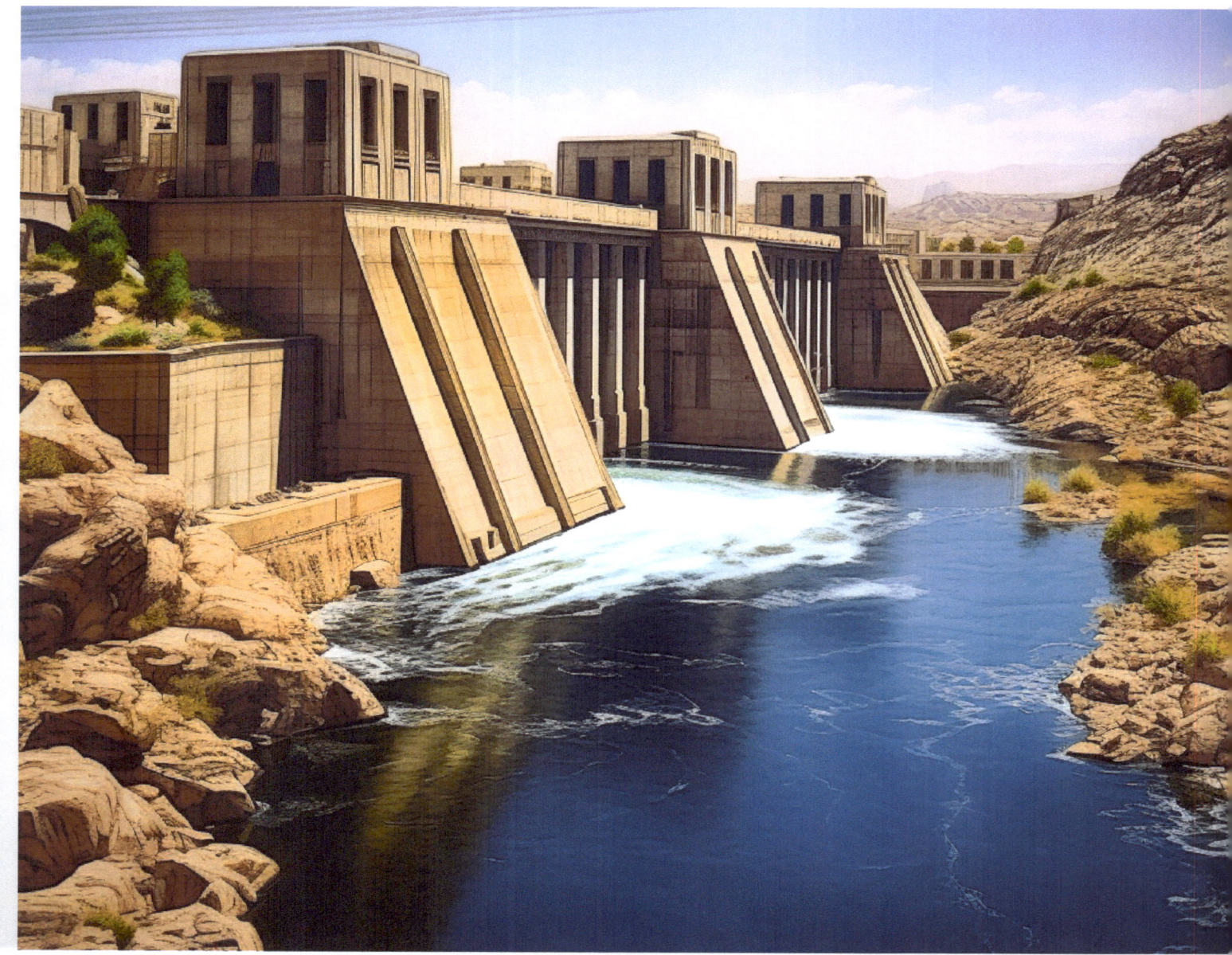

ASWAN HIGH DAM

A significant engineering project of the 20th century.

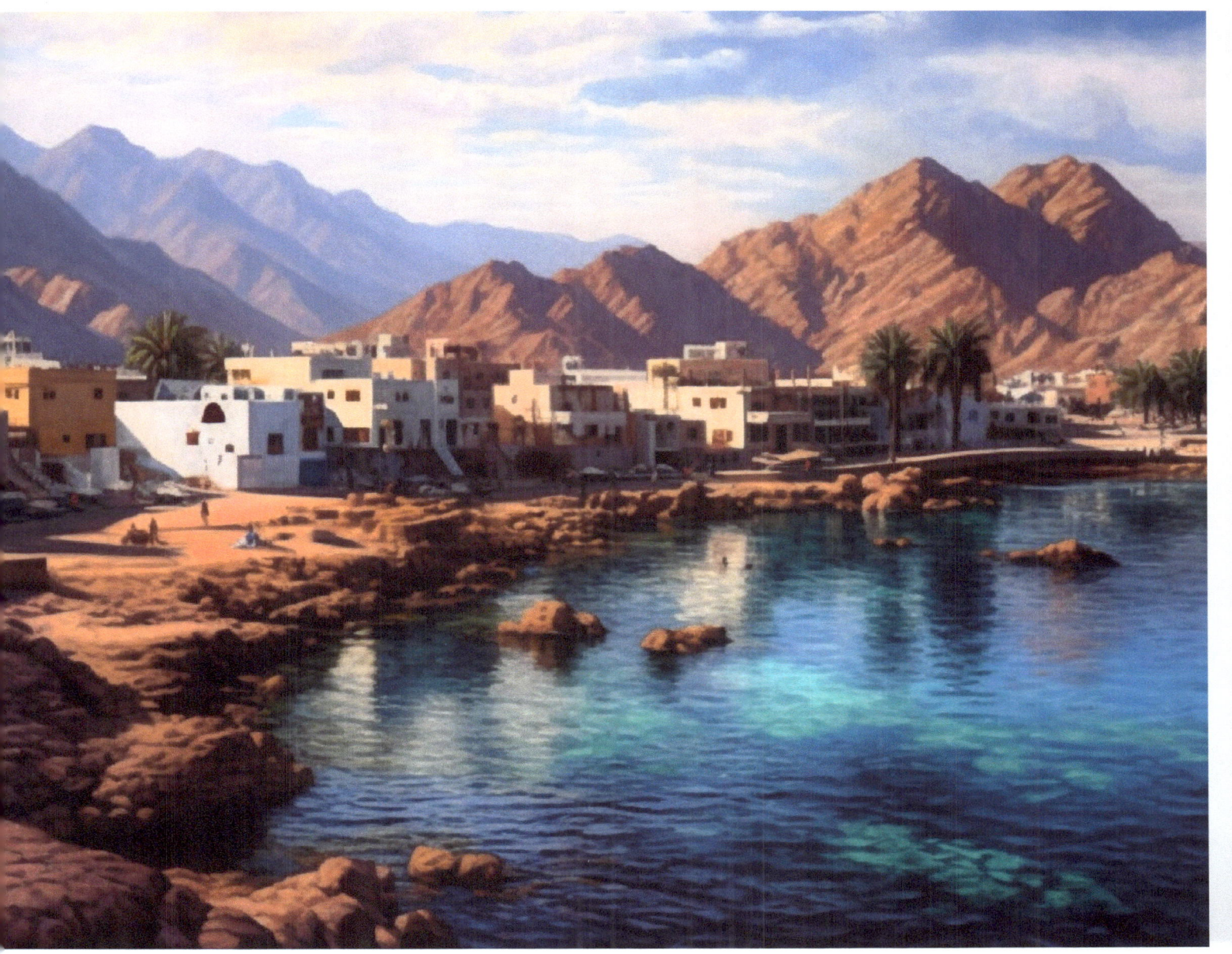

DAHAB

A small town on the southeast coast famous for its golden beaches.

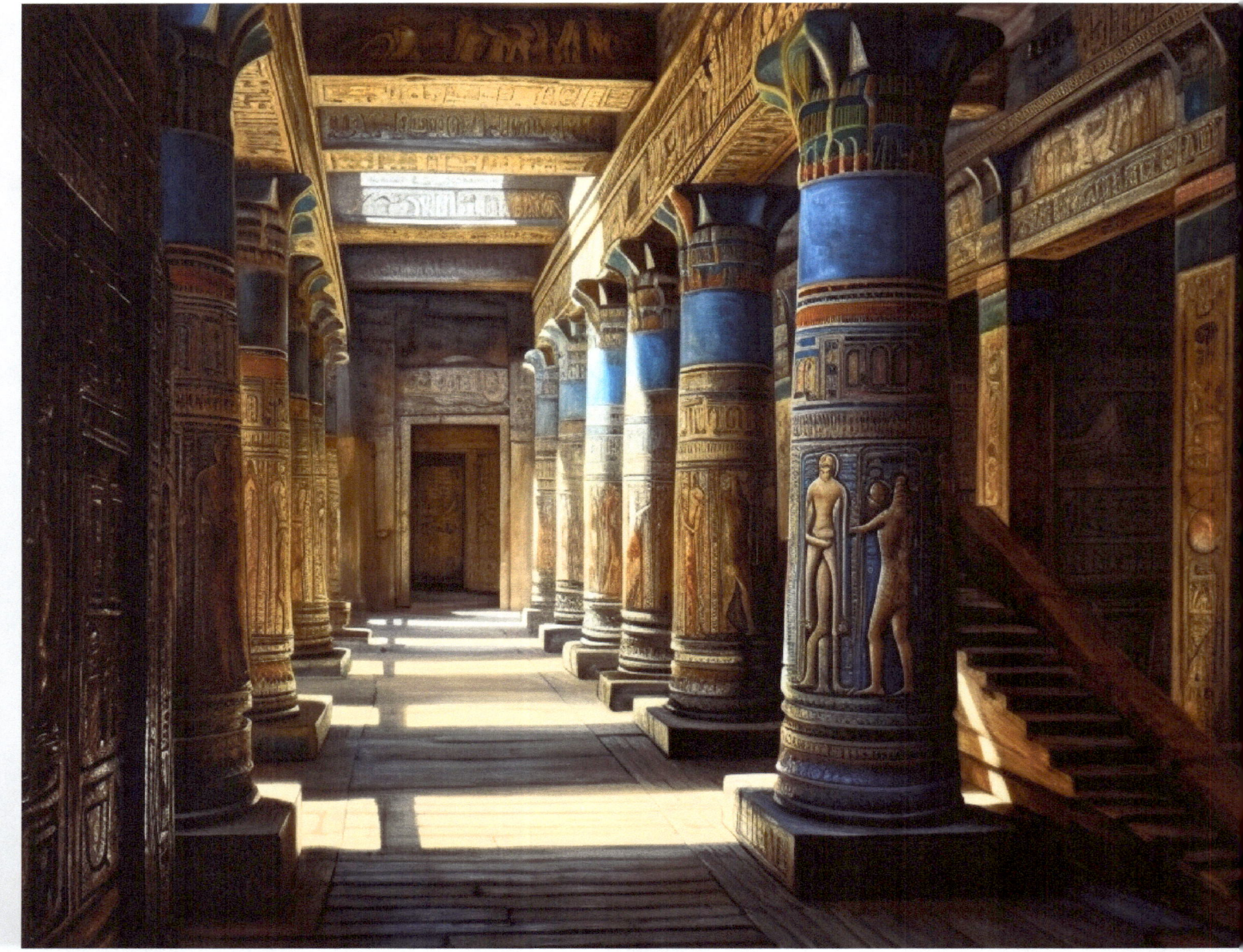

DENDERA TEMPLE COMPLEX

Houses one of the best-preserved temple complexes in Egypt.

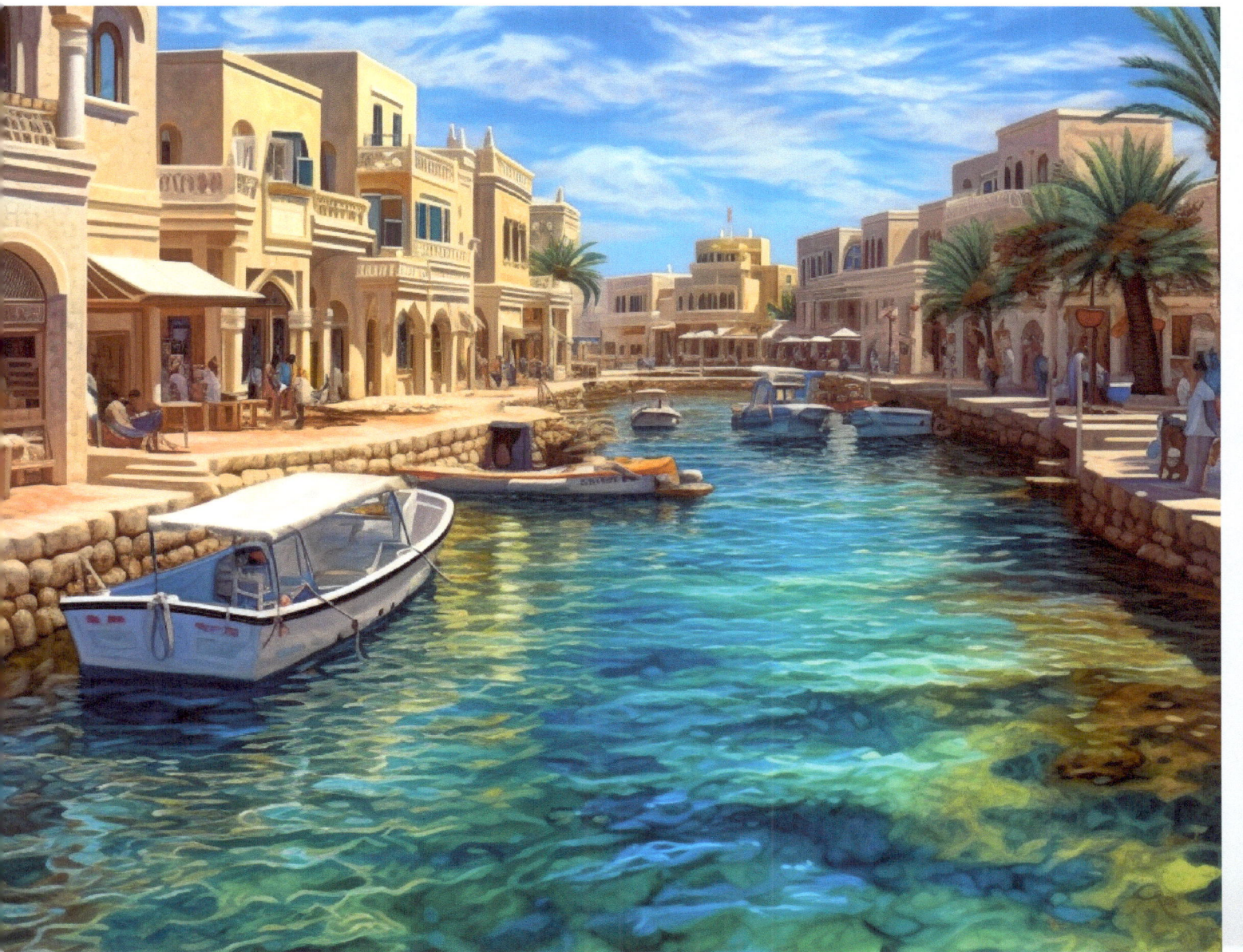

HURGHADA

A beach resort town along the Red Sea coast.

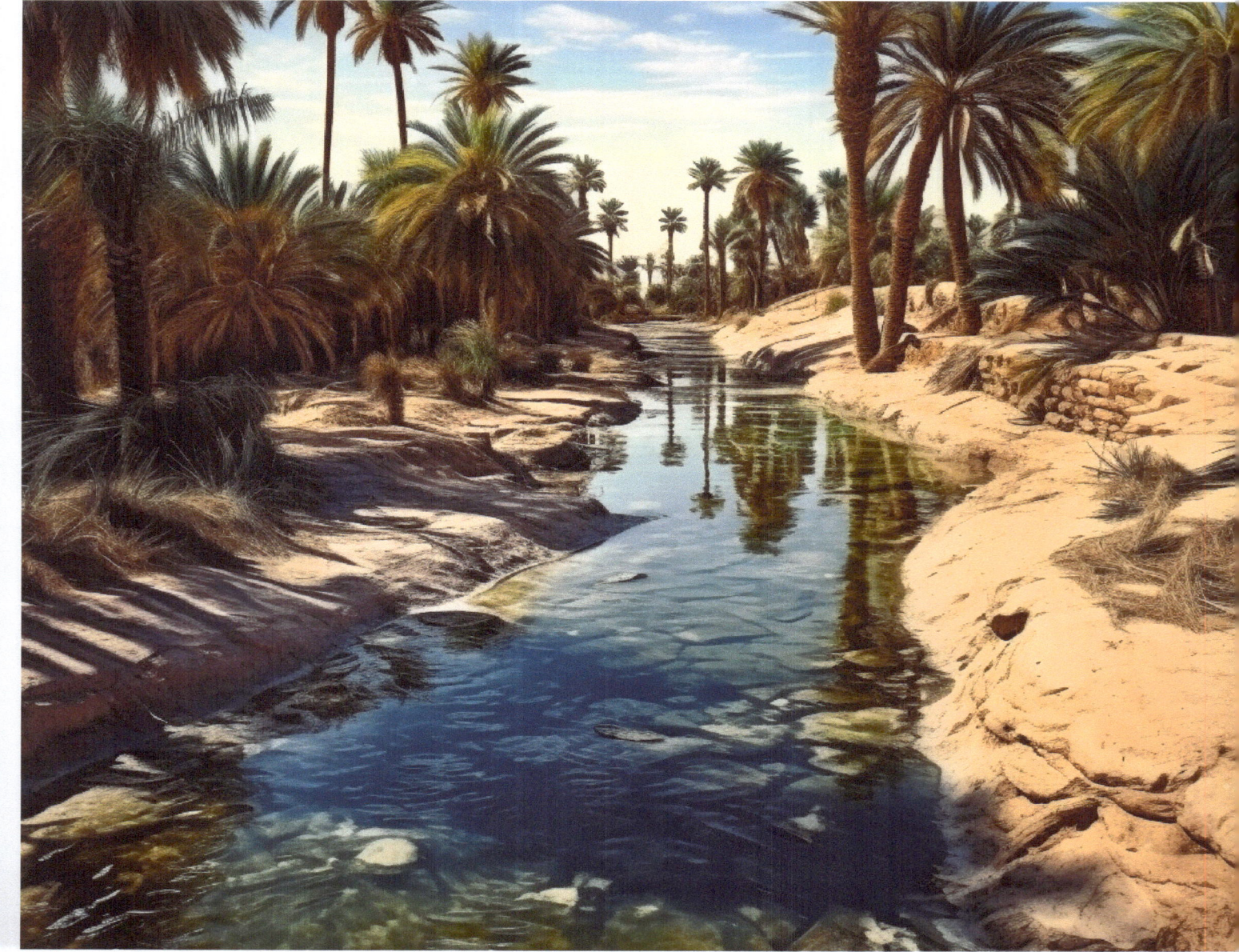

FAYOUM OASIS

Known for its lush palm groves and deep-blue lakes.

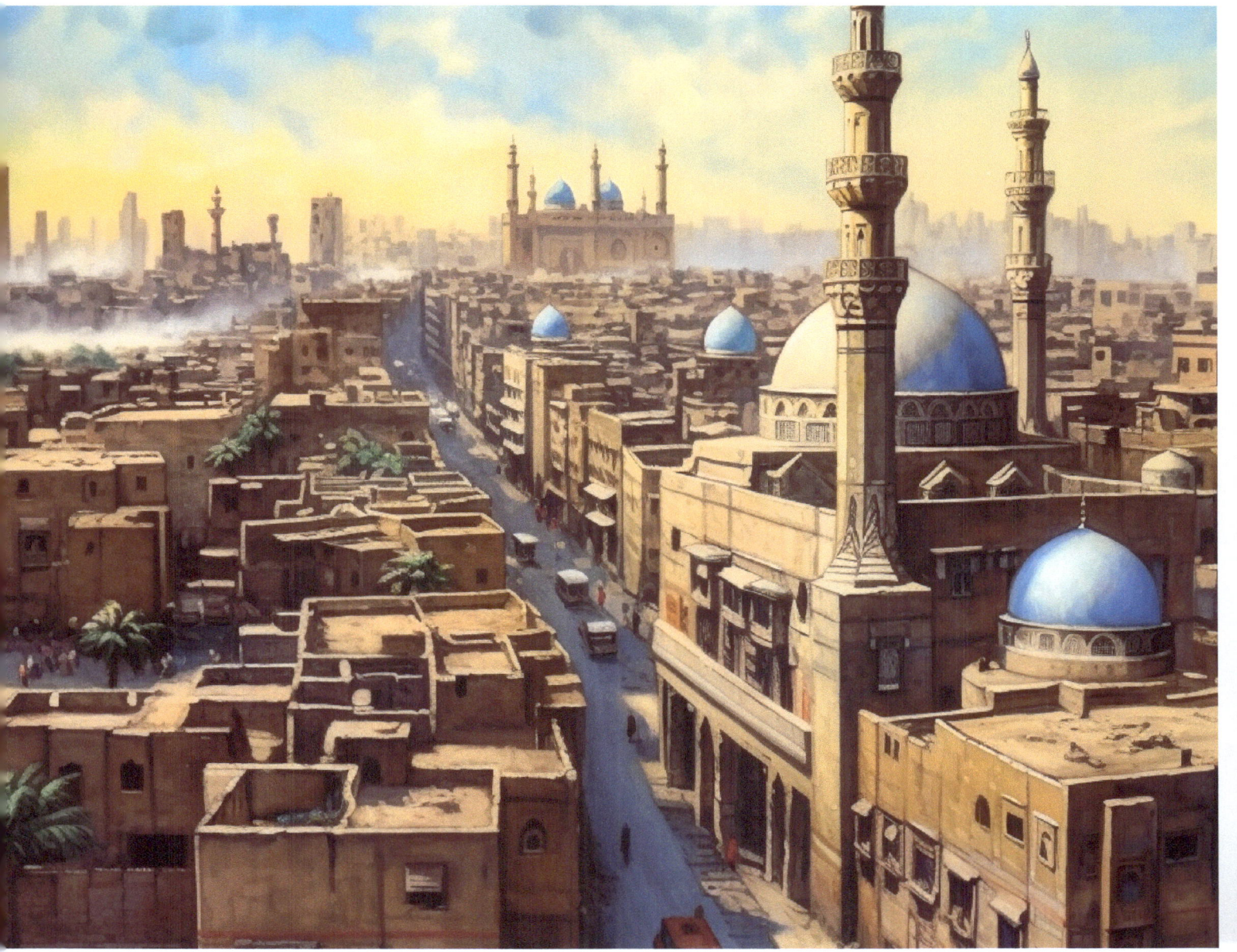

ISLAMIC CAIRO

Known for its historic mosques and Islamic structures.

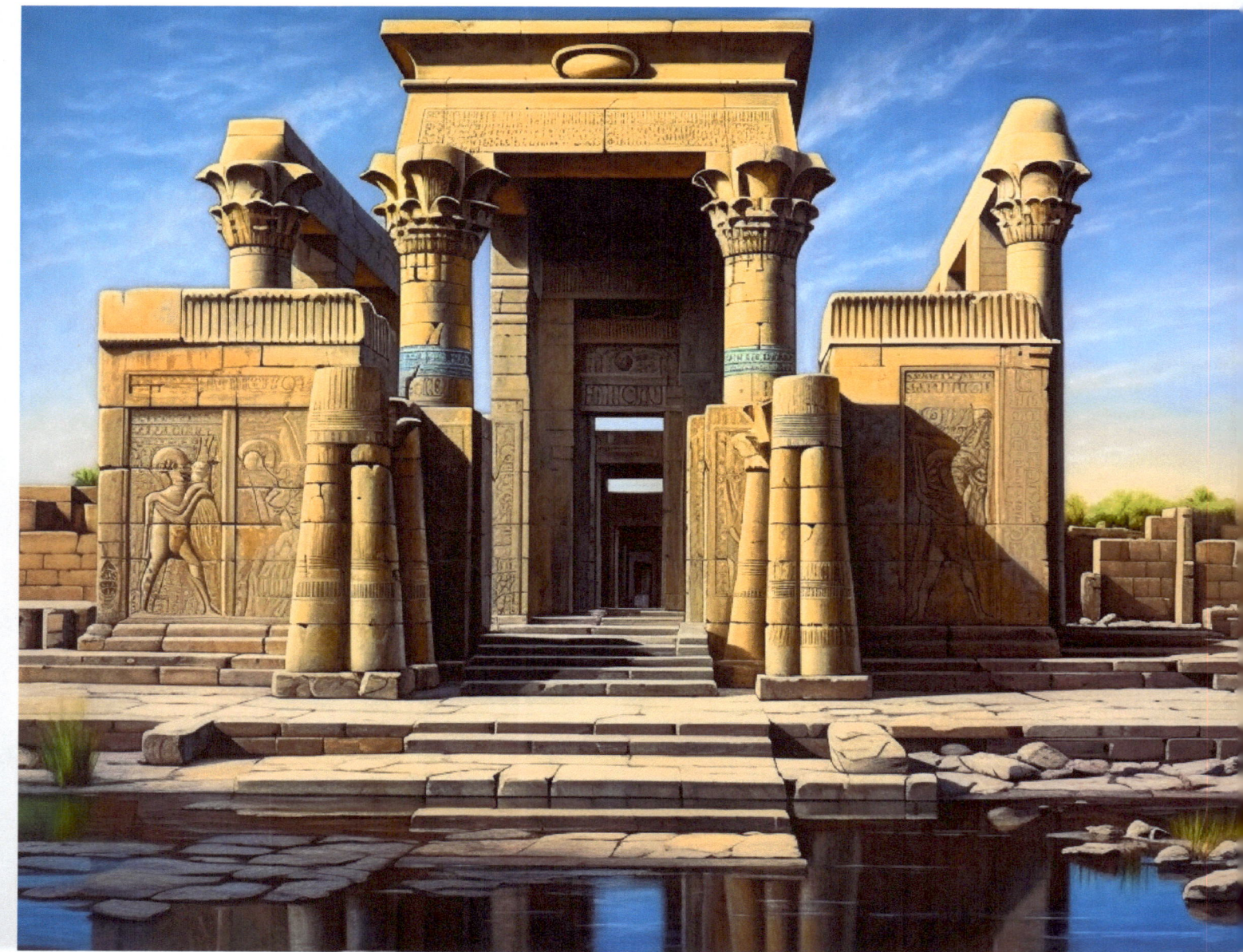

KOM OMBO TEMPLE

A unique double temple in the town of Kom Ombo.

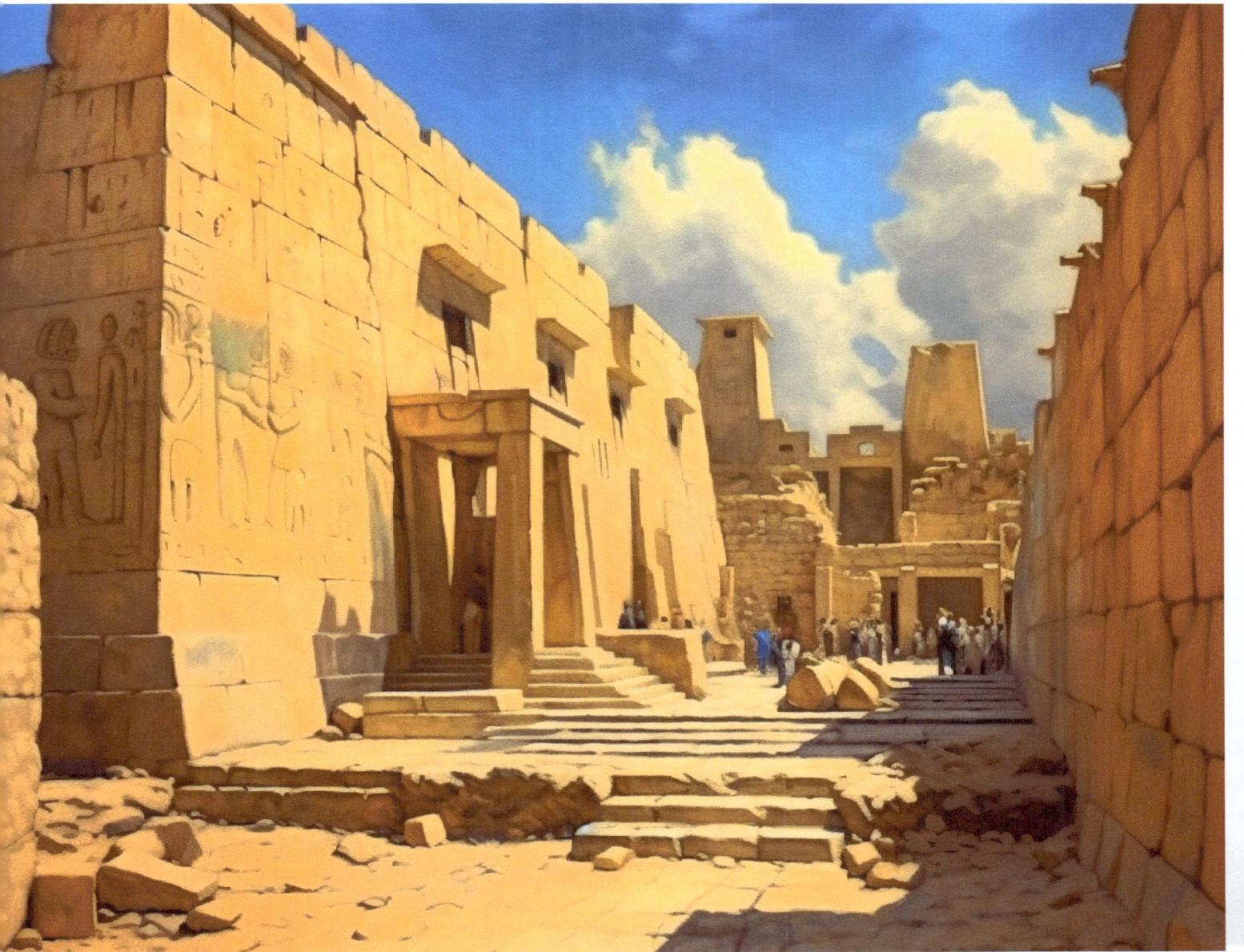

KARNAK TEMPLE COMPLEX

A collection of temples, chapels, pylons, and other buildings
in Luxor.

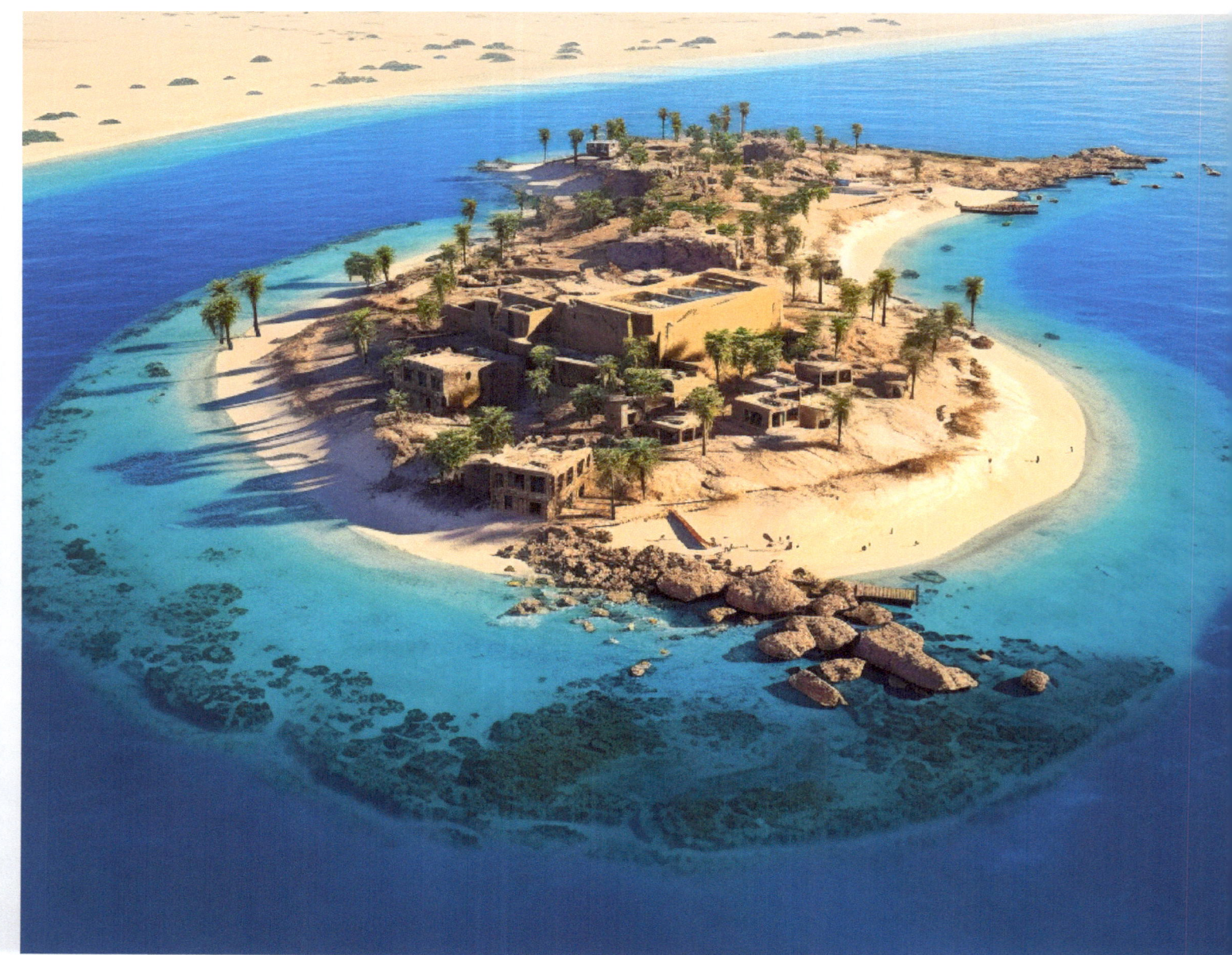

MAHMYA ISLAND

A protected area of the Red Sea with beautiful beaches.

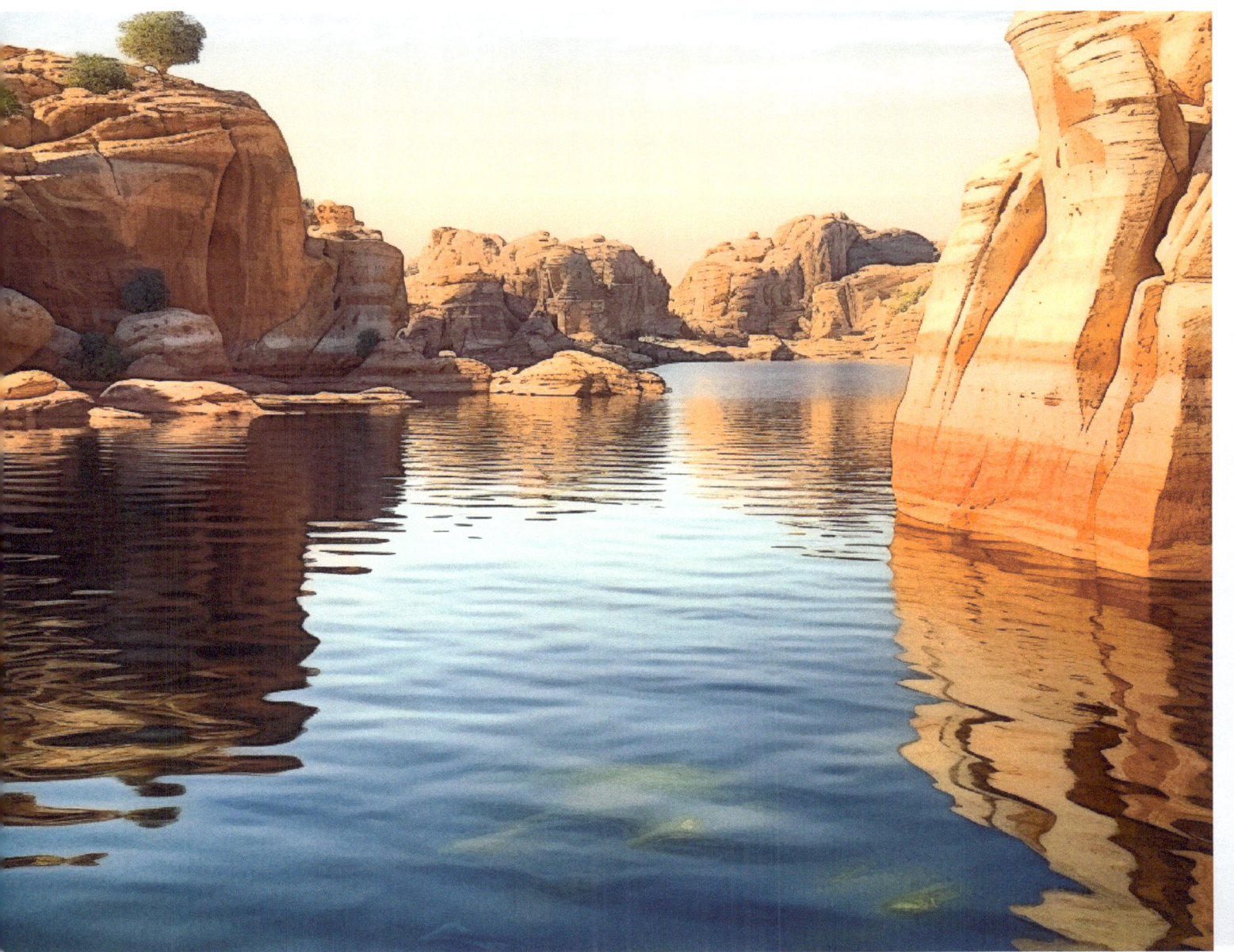

LAKE NASSER

One of the largest artificial lakes in the world.

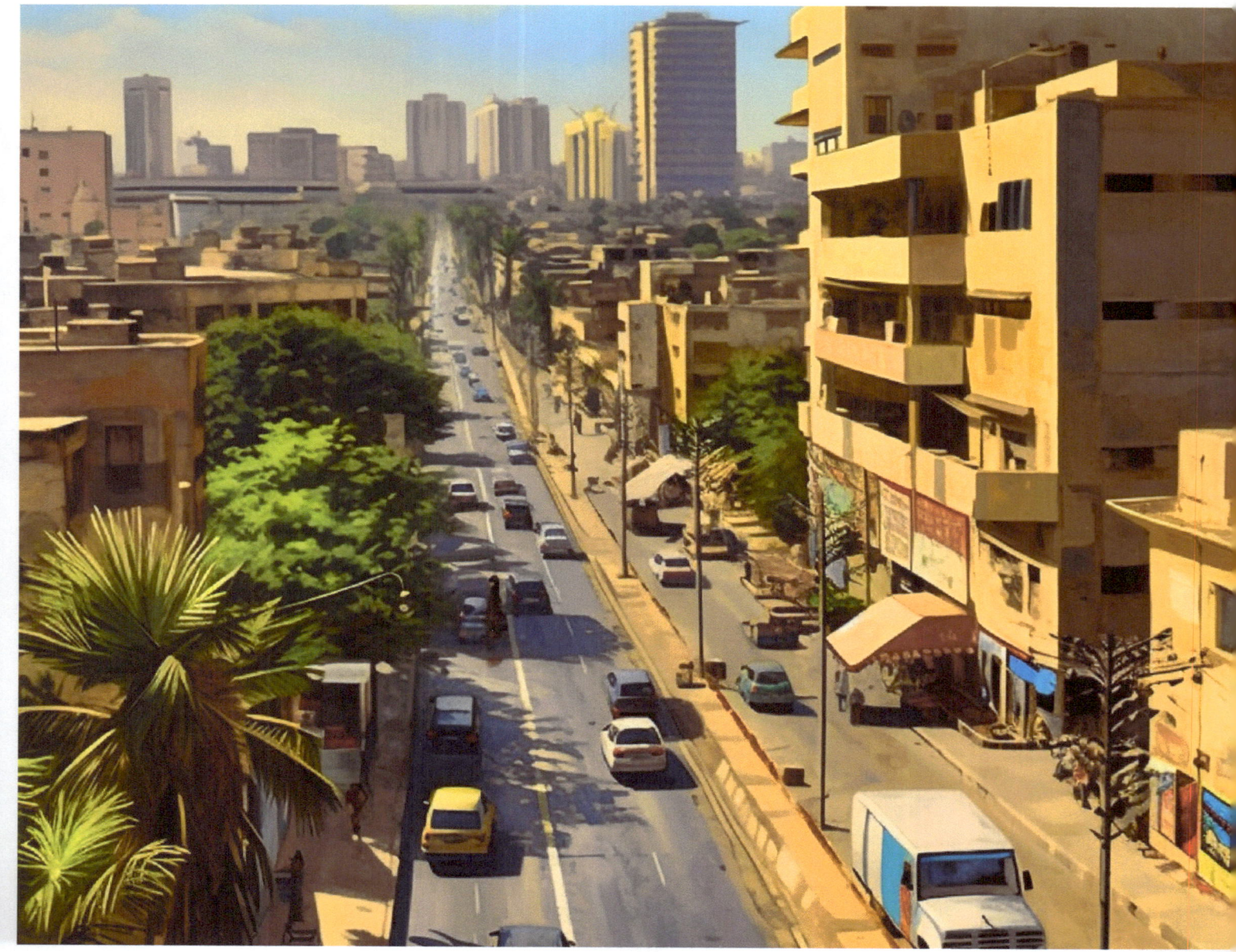

MEMPHIS

The ancient capital of Egypt, with various statues of Ramses
II.

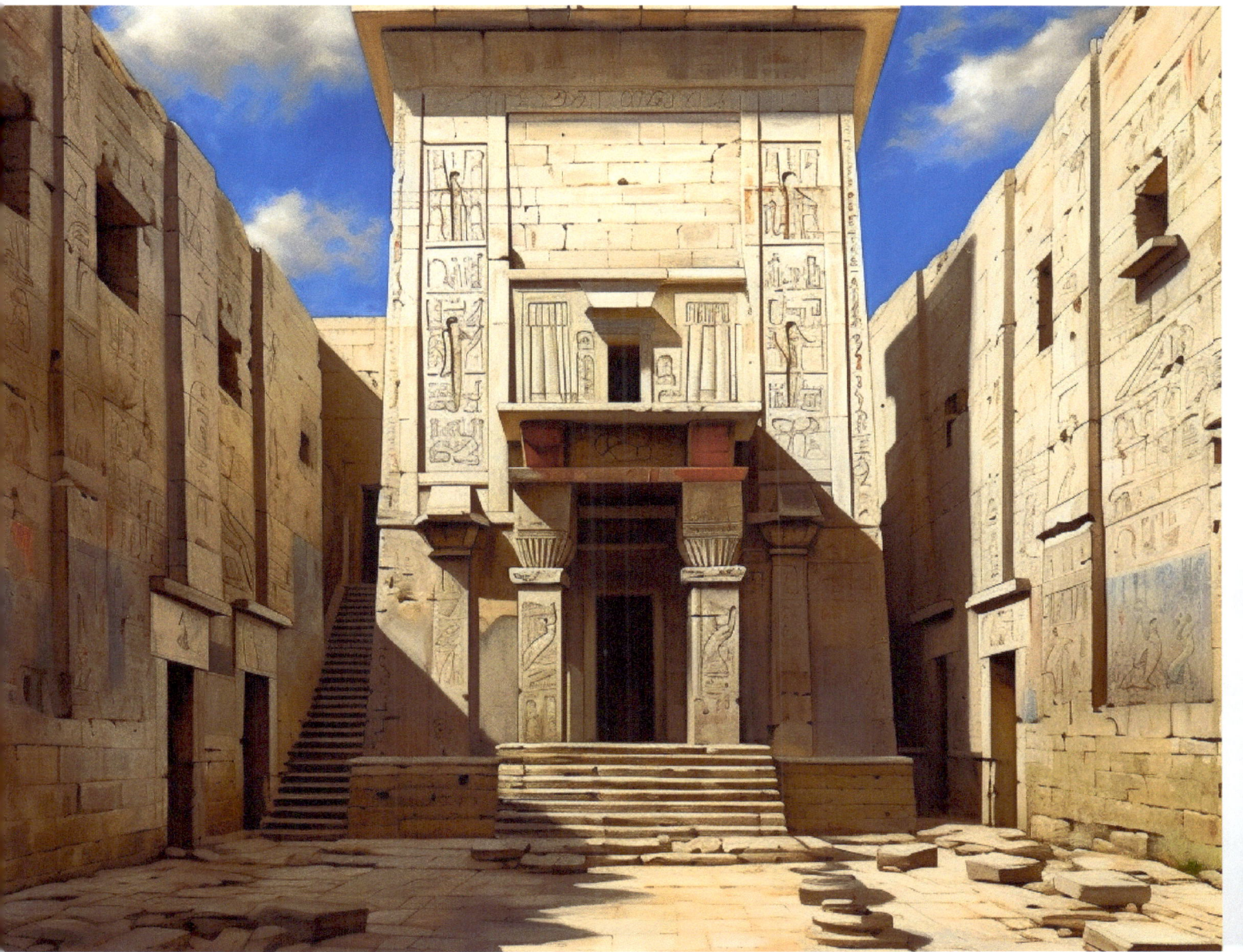

MEDINET HABU

A large temple complex second only in size to the Karnak Temple.

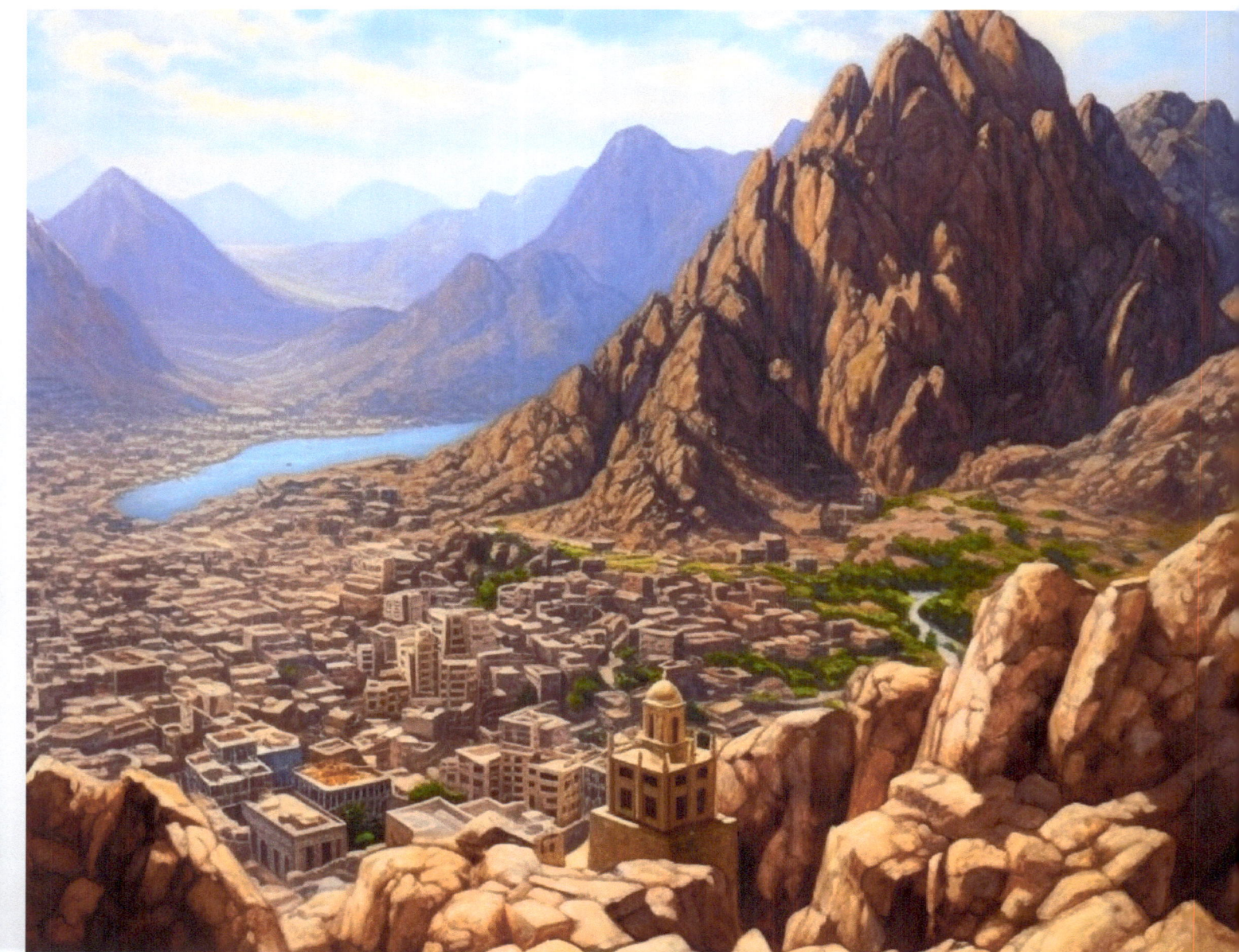

MOUNT SINAI

A significant religious site and a place for hiking.

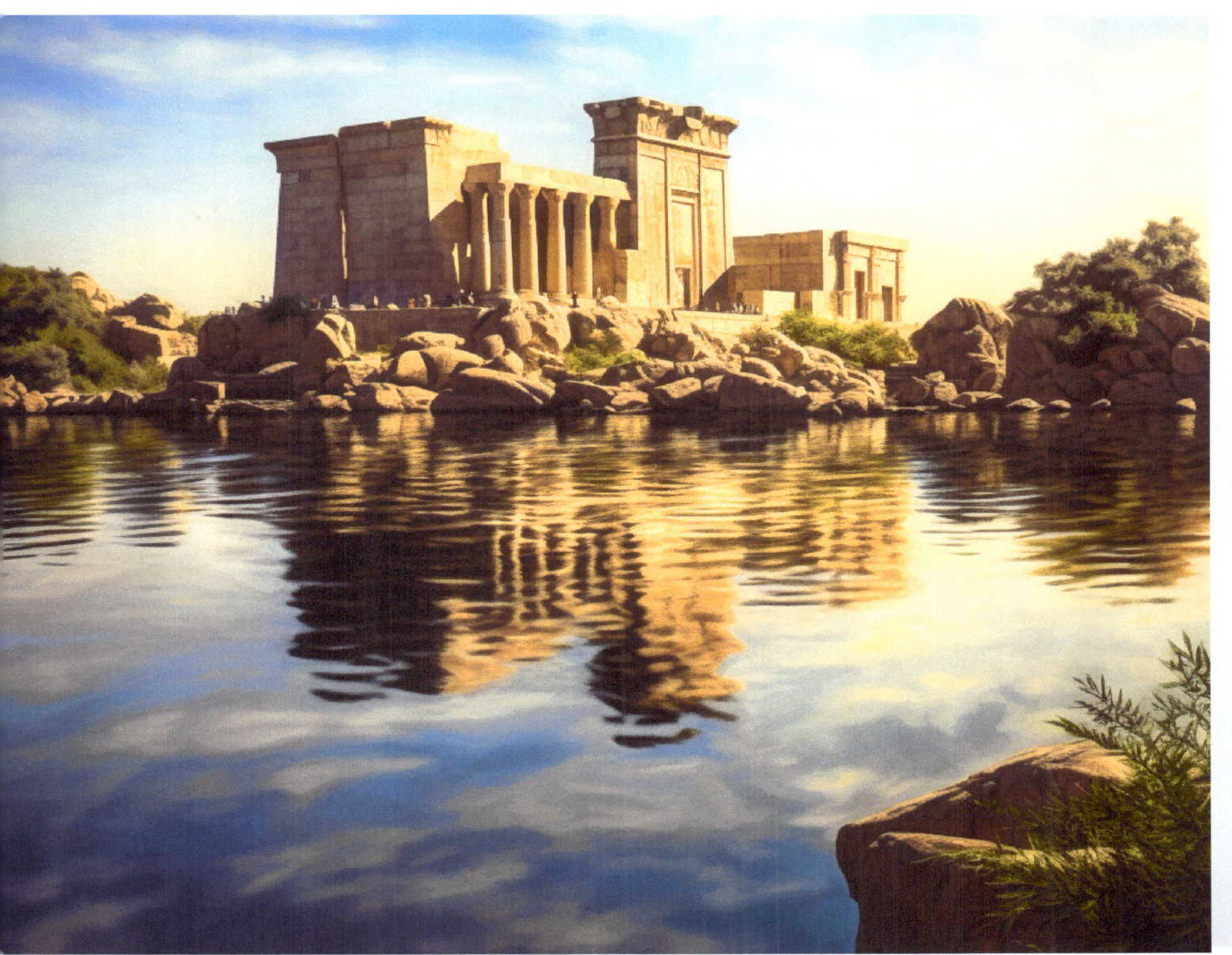

PHILAE TEMPLE

A temple complex dedicated to the goddess Isis.

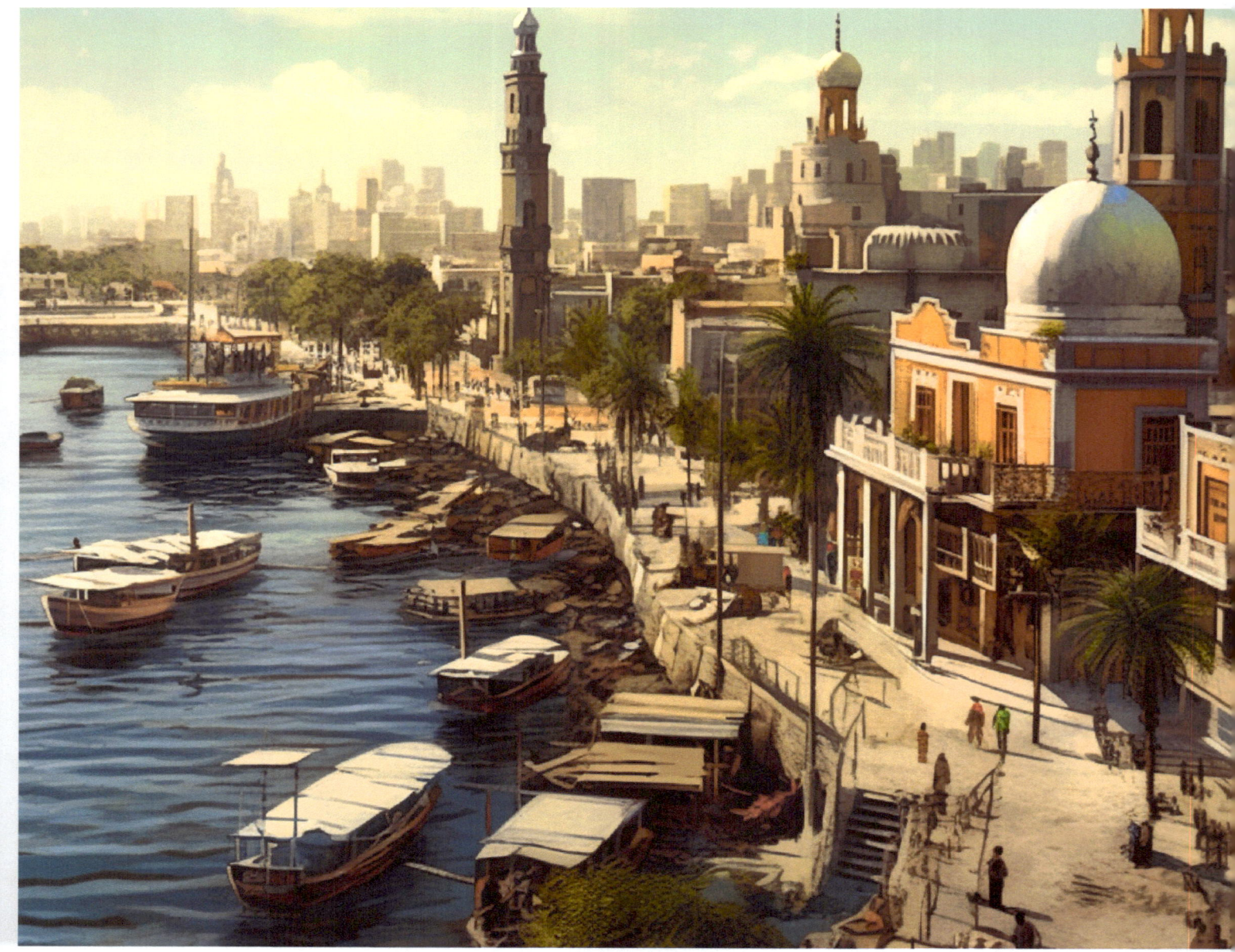

PORT SAID

Known for its lighthouse and as the northern gateway to the
Suez Canal.

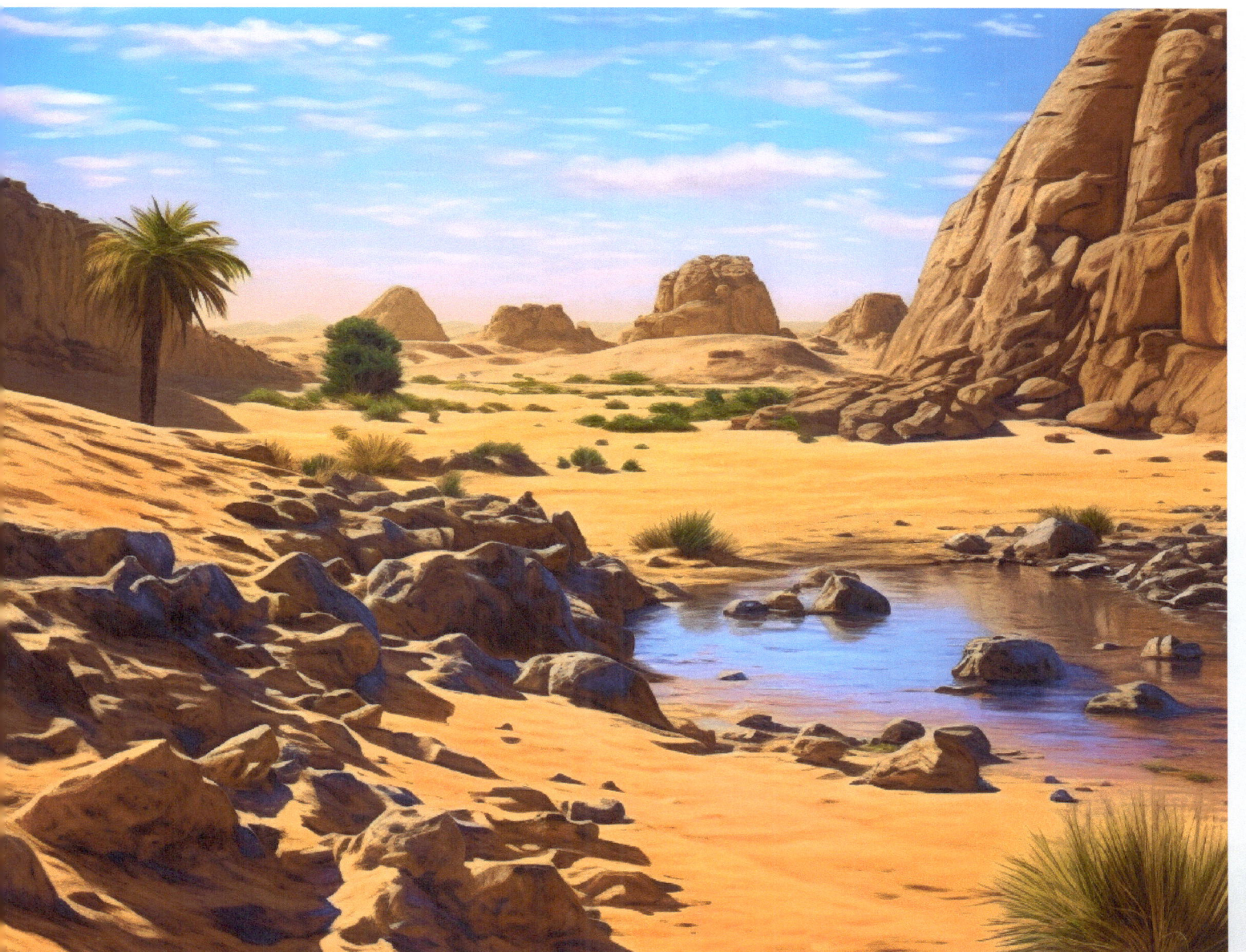

RAS MOHAMMED NATIONAL PARK

Known for its stunning snorkeling and diving locations.

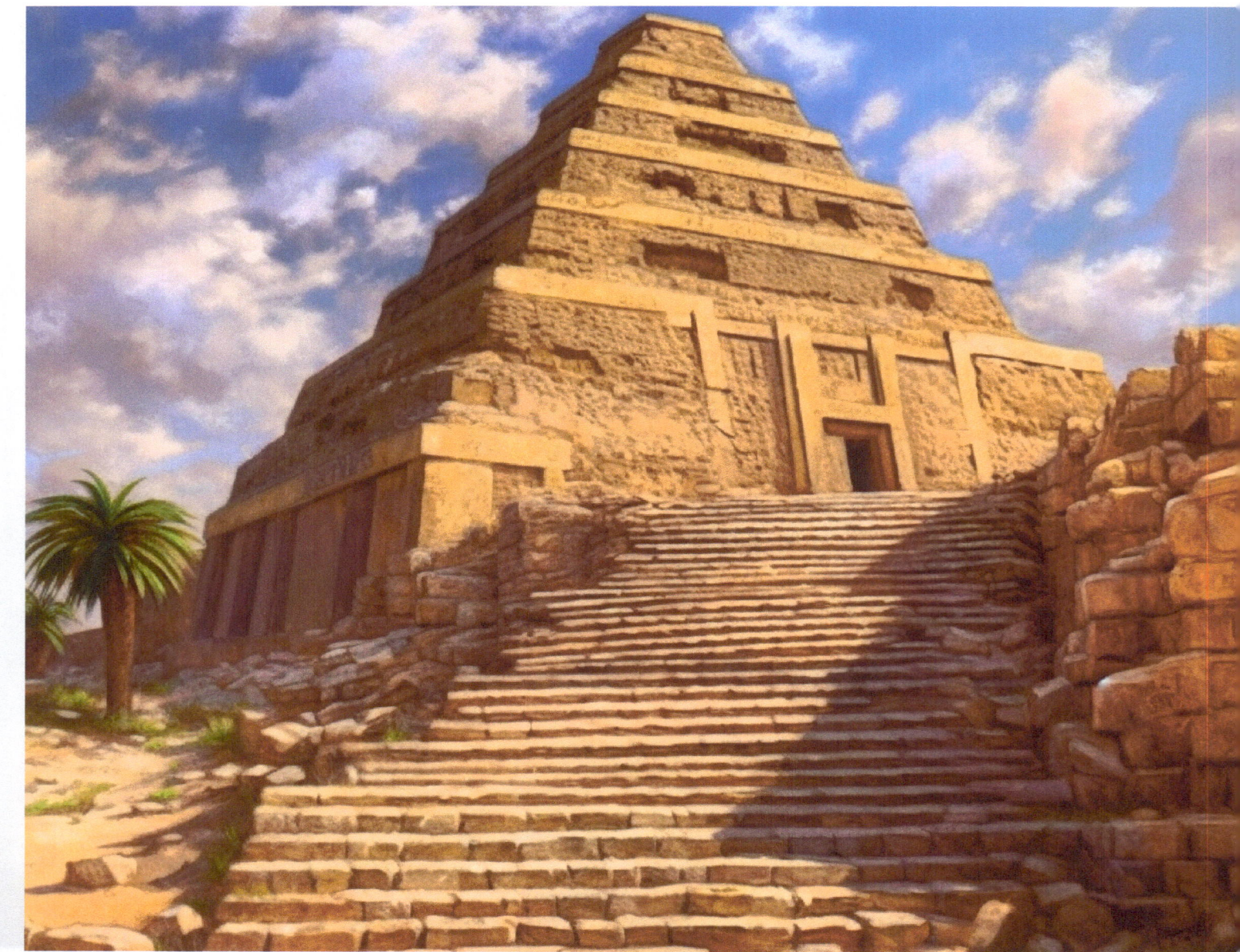

SAQQARA

A vast ancient burial ground in Egypt.

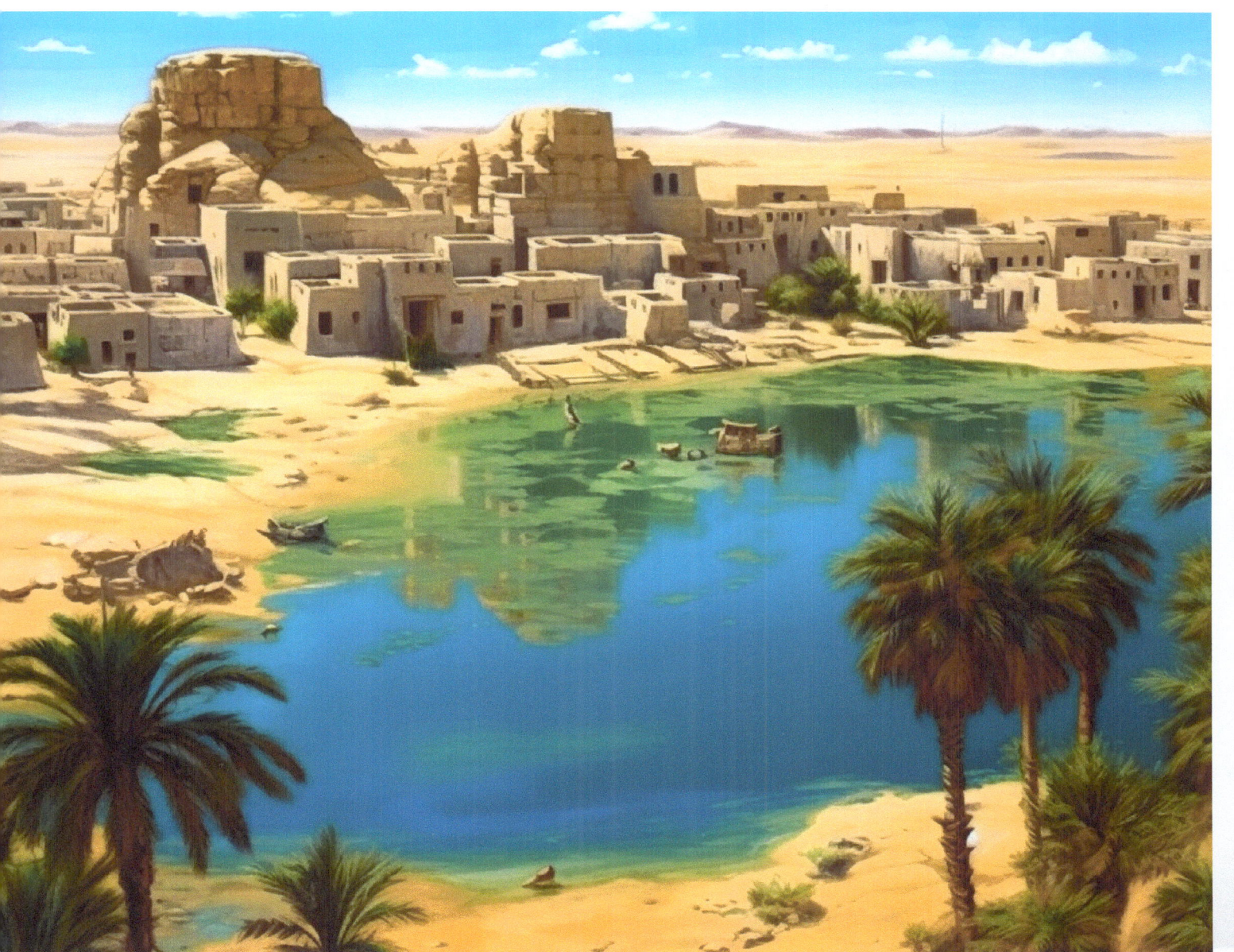

SIWA OASIS

An isolated oasis with a rich cultural history.

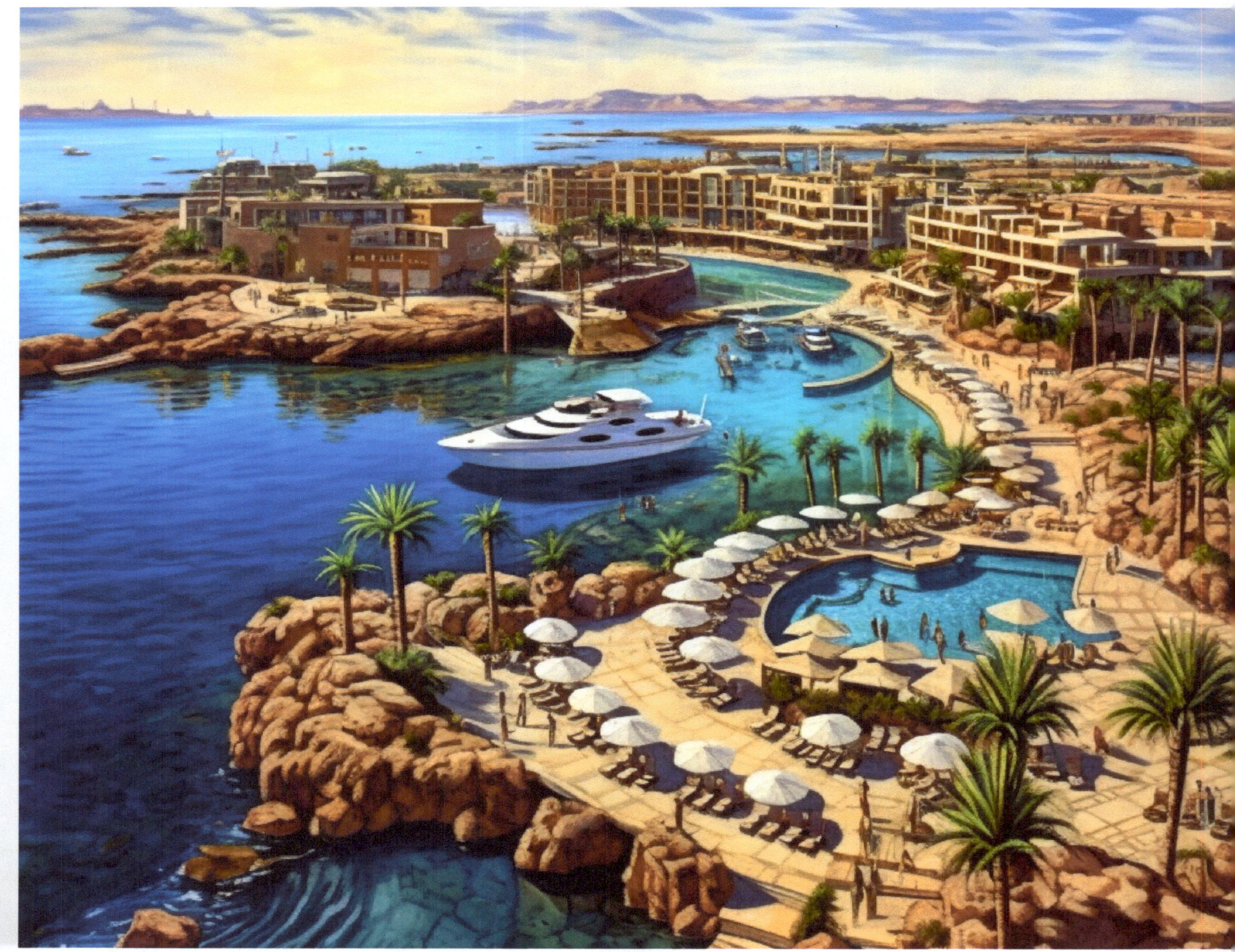

SHARM EL SHEIKH

Known for its sheltered sandy beaches, clear waters, and diving sites.

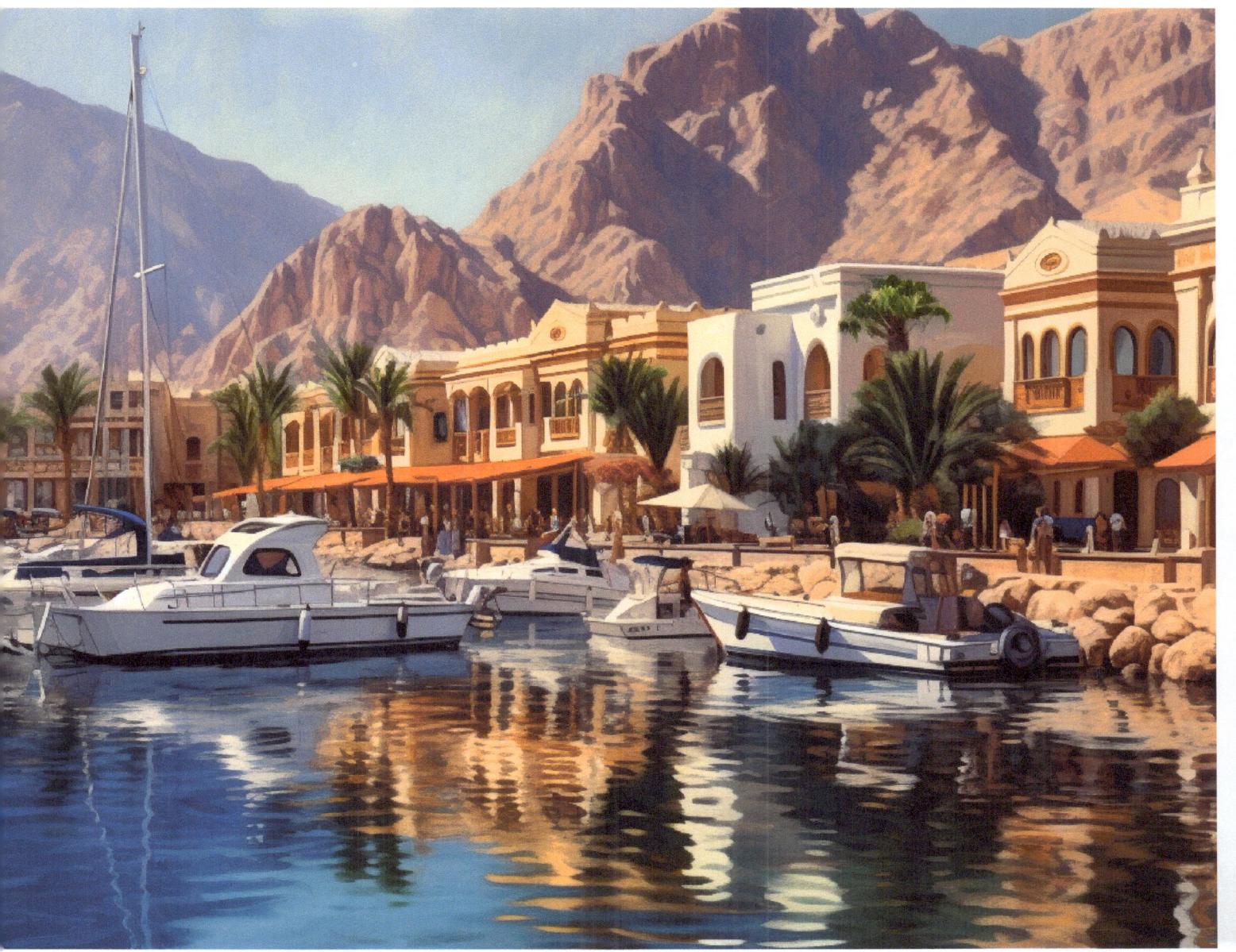

TABA

A resort town near the northern tip of the Gulf of Aqaba.

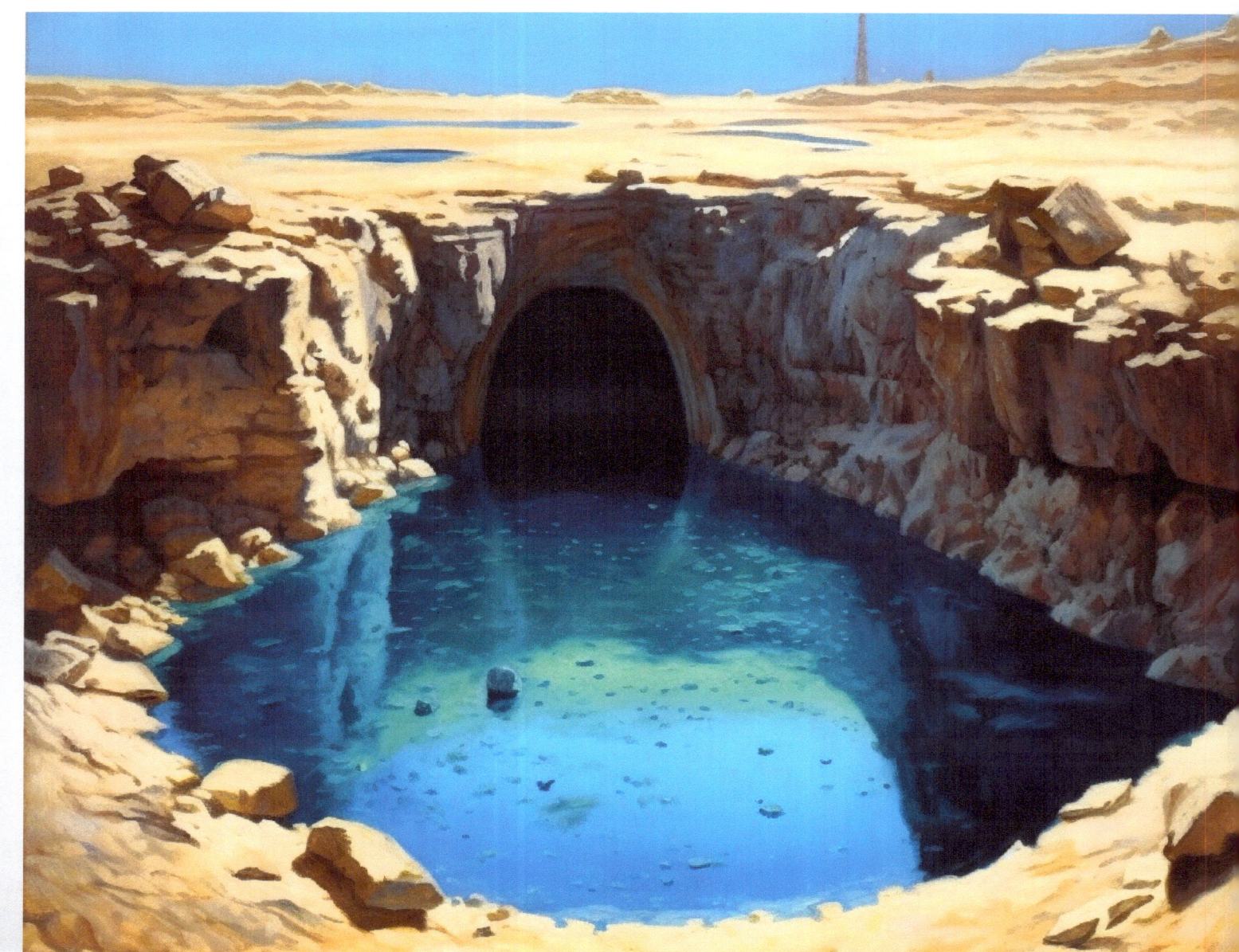

THE BLUE HOLE

A renowned diving location near Dahab.

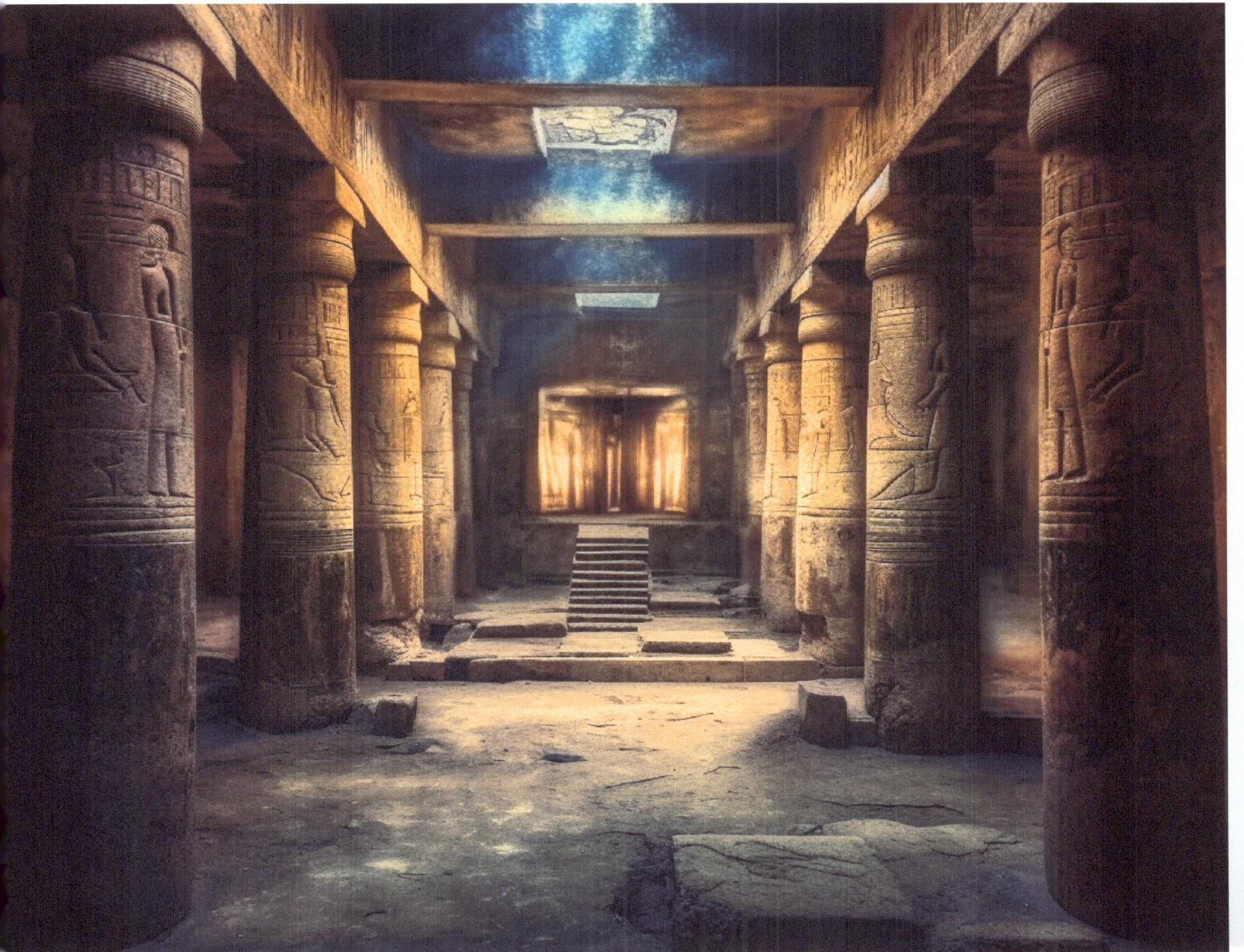

CATACOMBS OF KOM EL SHOQAFA

A series of Alexandrian tombs, statues, and archaeological objects.

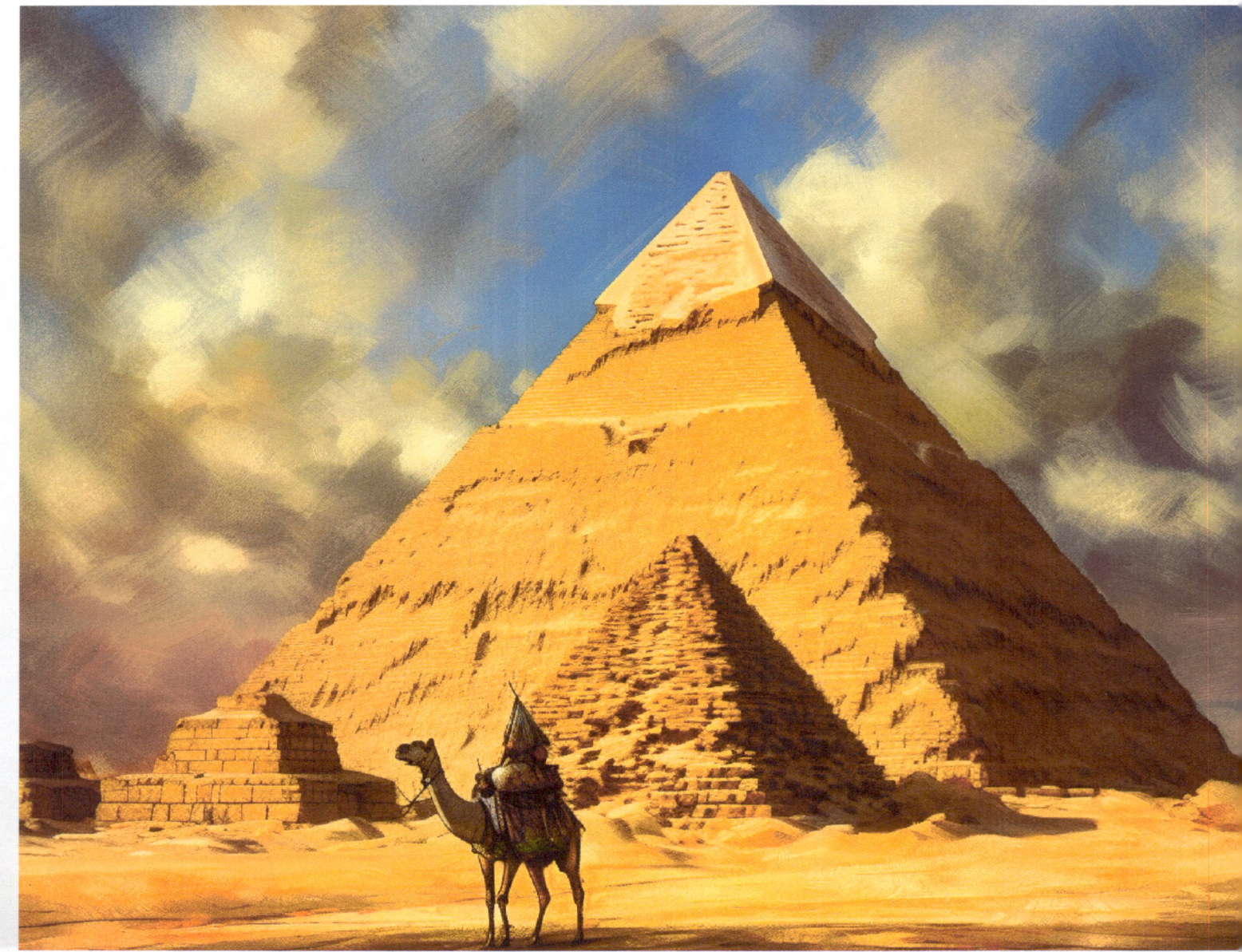

GREAT PYRAMIDS OF GIZA

Iconic structures and one of the Seven Wonders of the Ancient World.

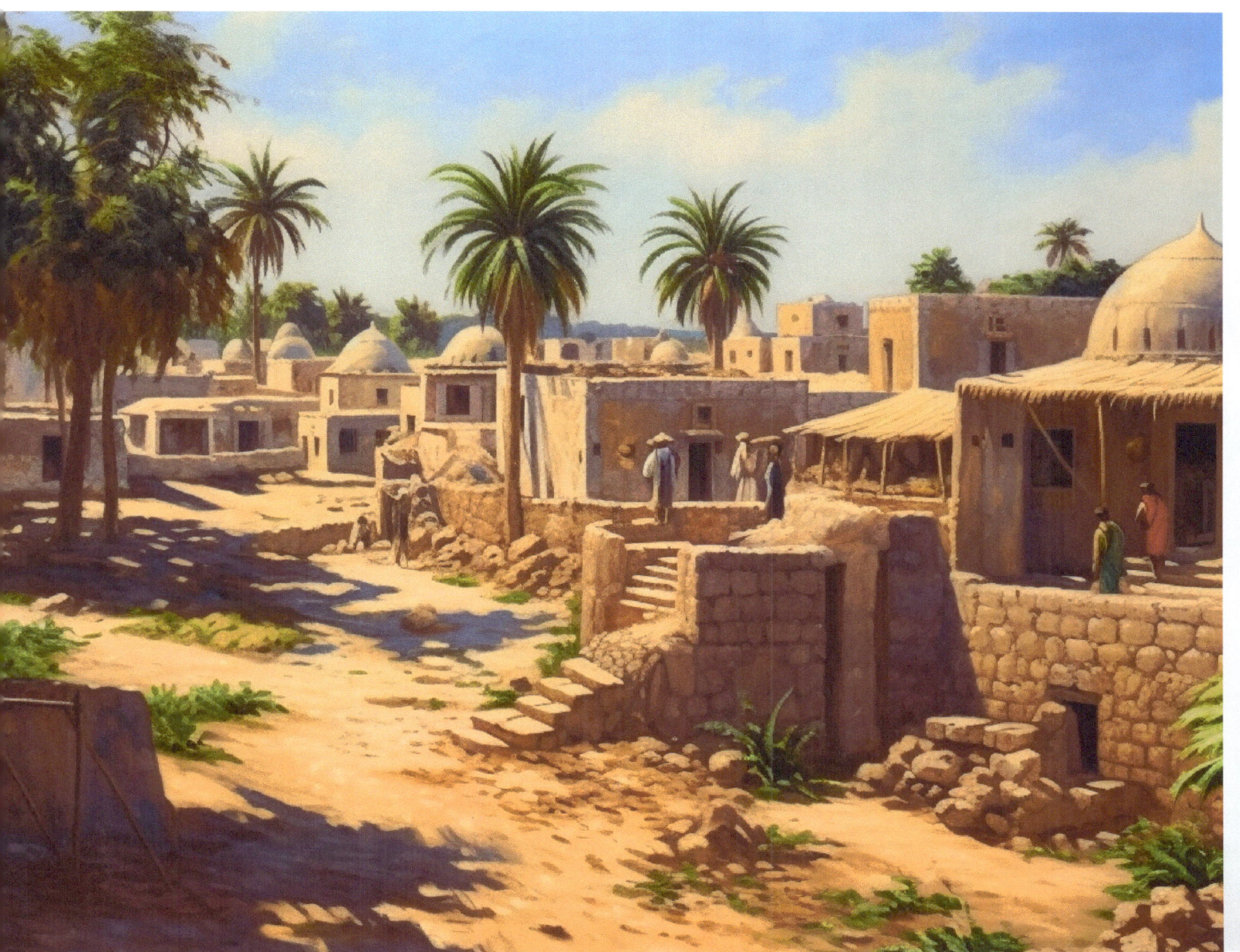

THE NUBIAN VILLAGE

A colorful and culturally rich area near Aswan.

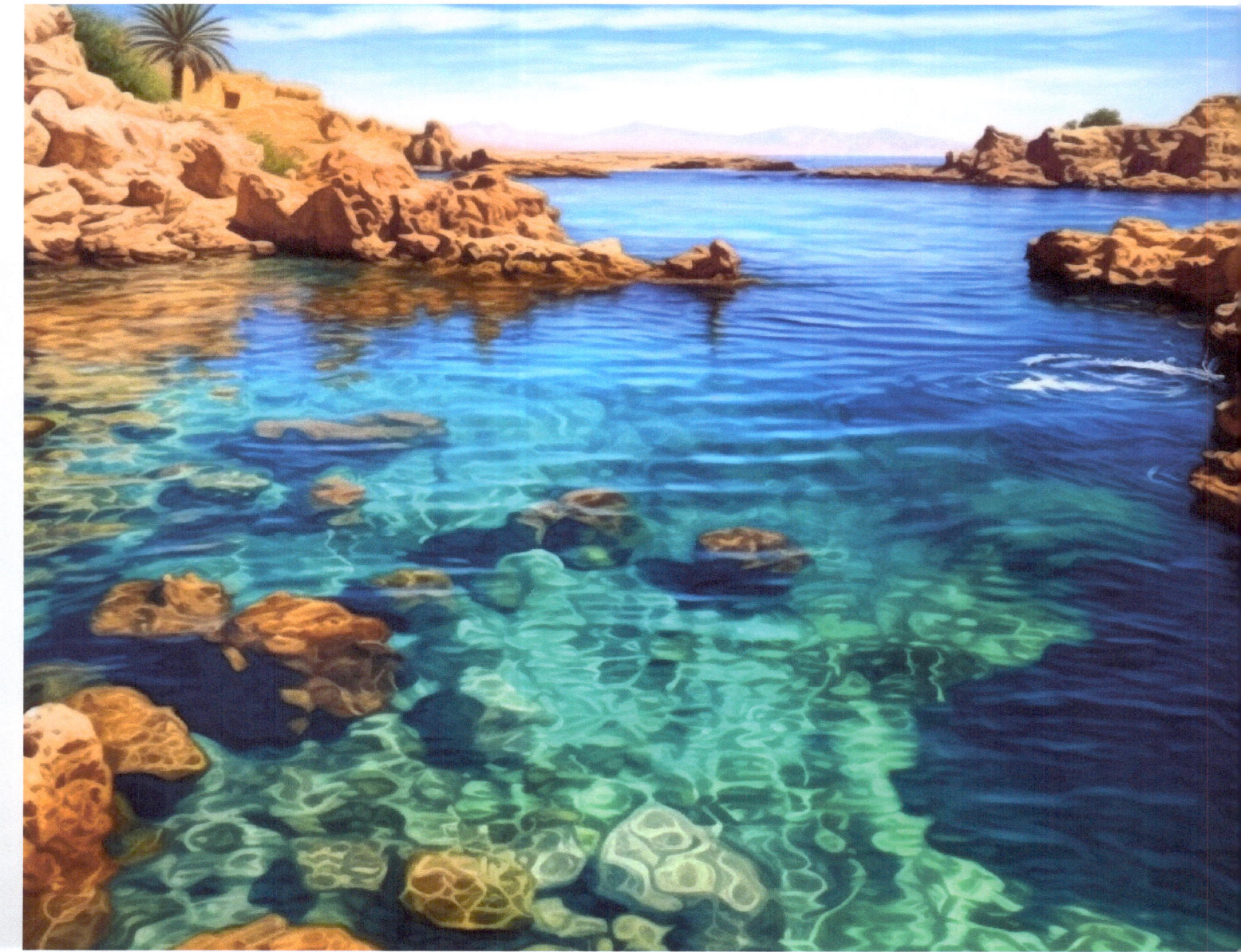

THE RED SEA RIVIERA

Famous for its vibrant marine life and beautiful coral reefs.

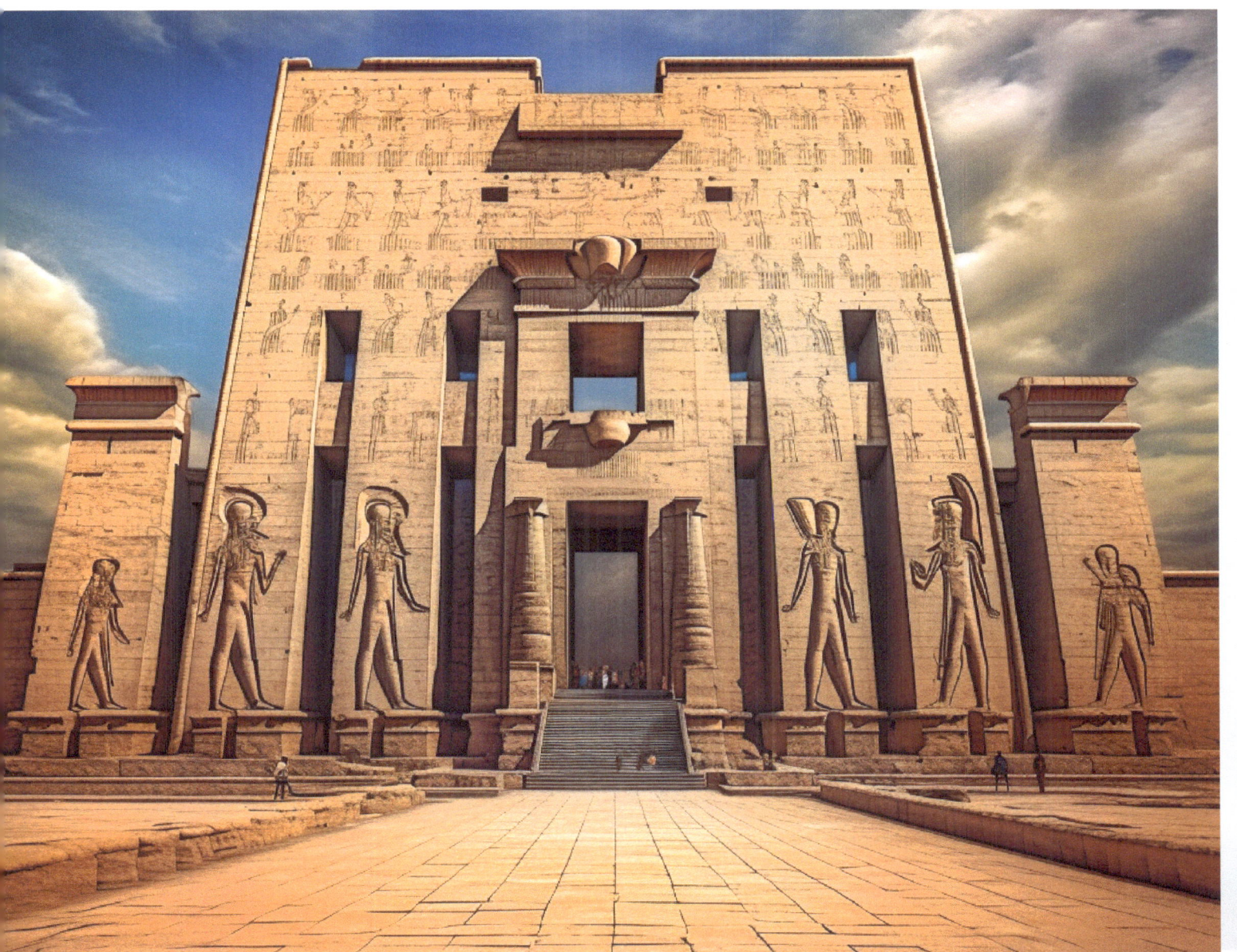

THE TEMPLE OF HORUS AT EDFU

A beautifully preserved Ptolemaic temple.

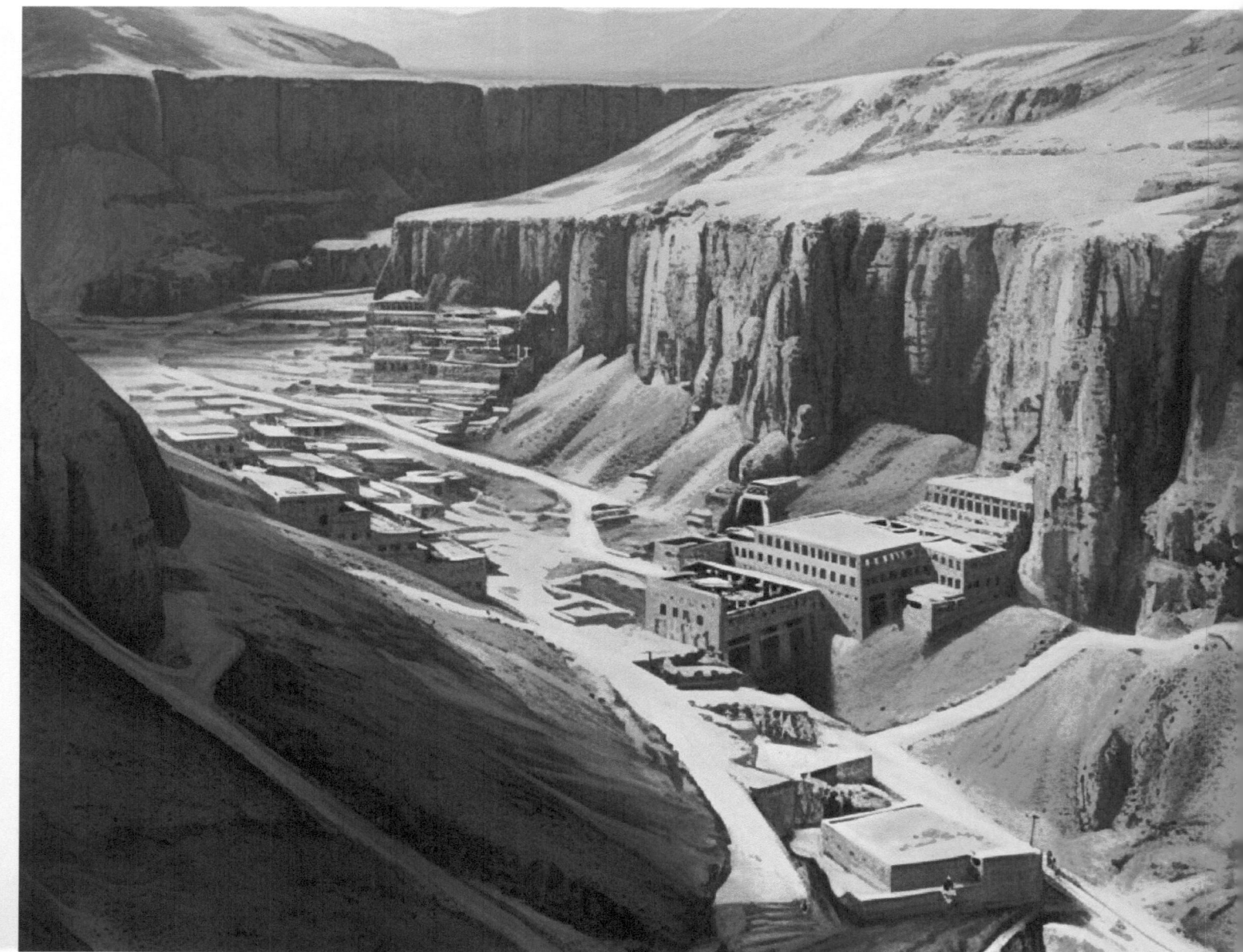

VALLEY OF THE KINGS
The burial place of Egypt's pharaohs and powerful nobles.

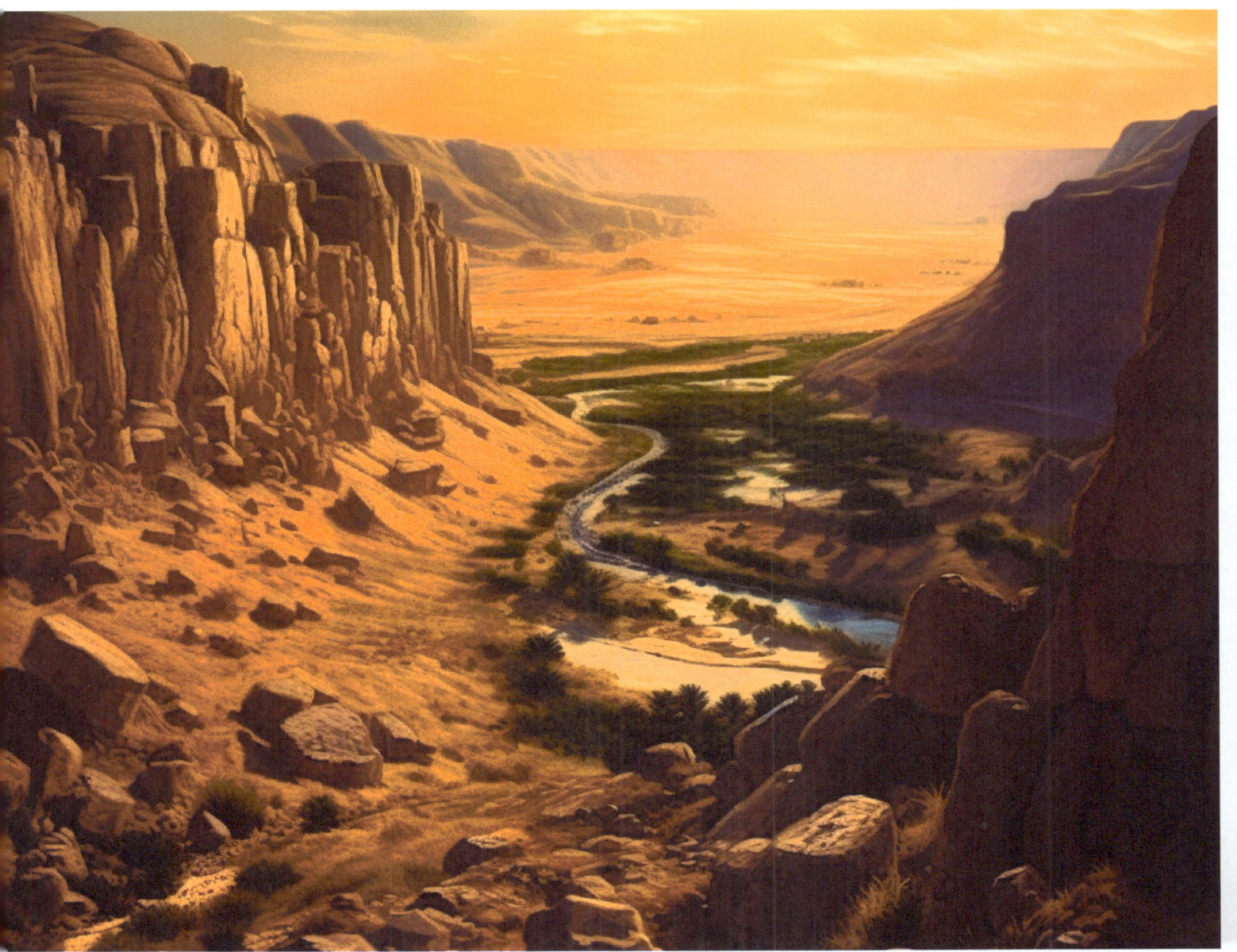

VALLEY OF THE QUEENS

A burial site for wives of pharaohs, princes, and princesses.

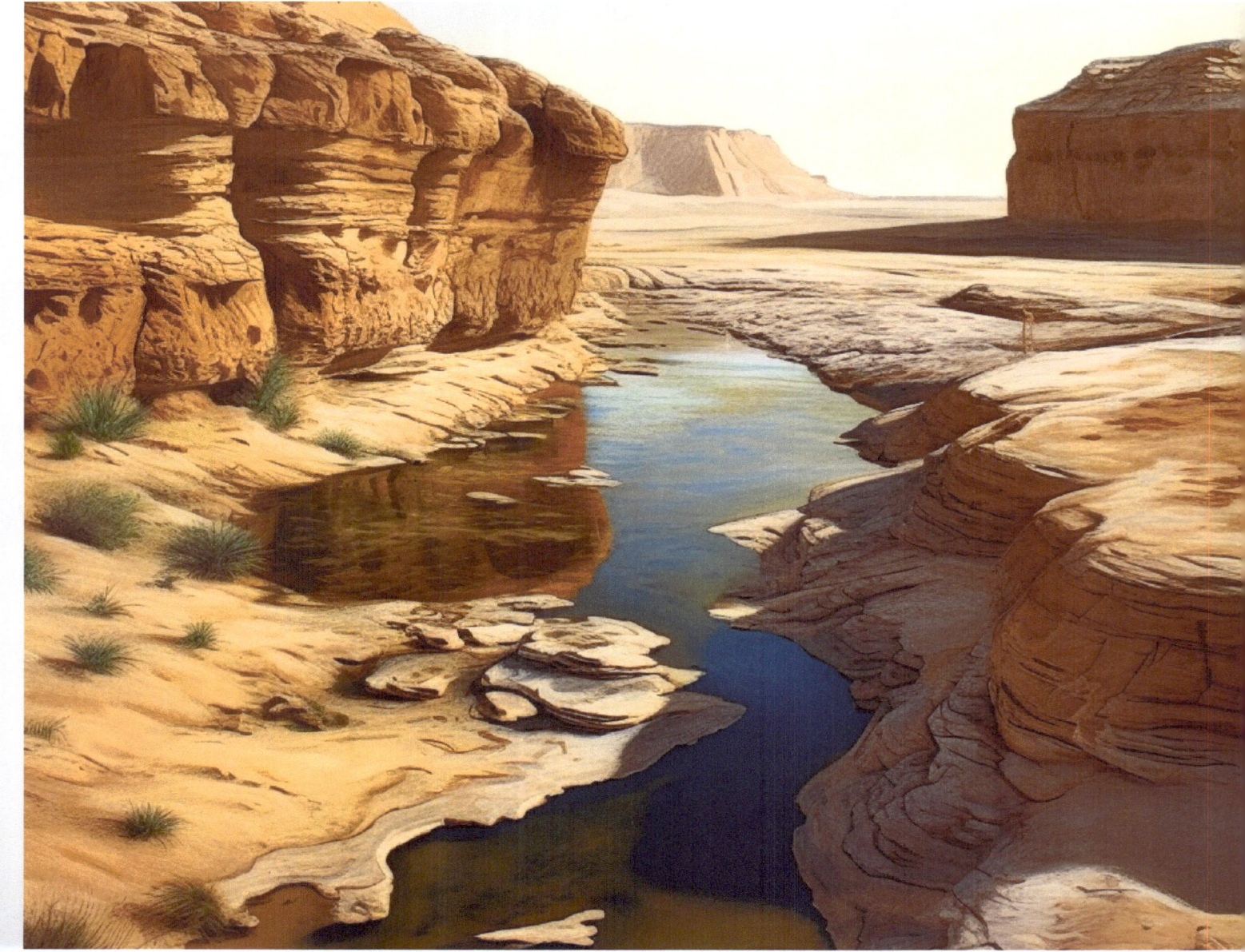

WADI EL HITAN

A paleontological site in the Al Fayyum Governorate.

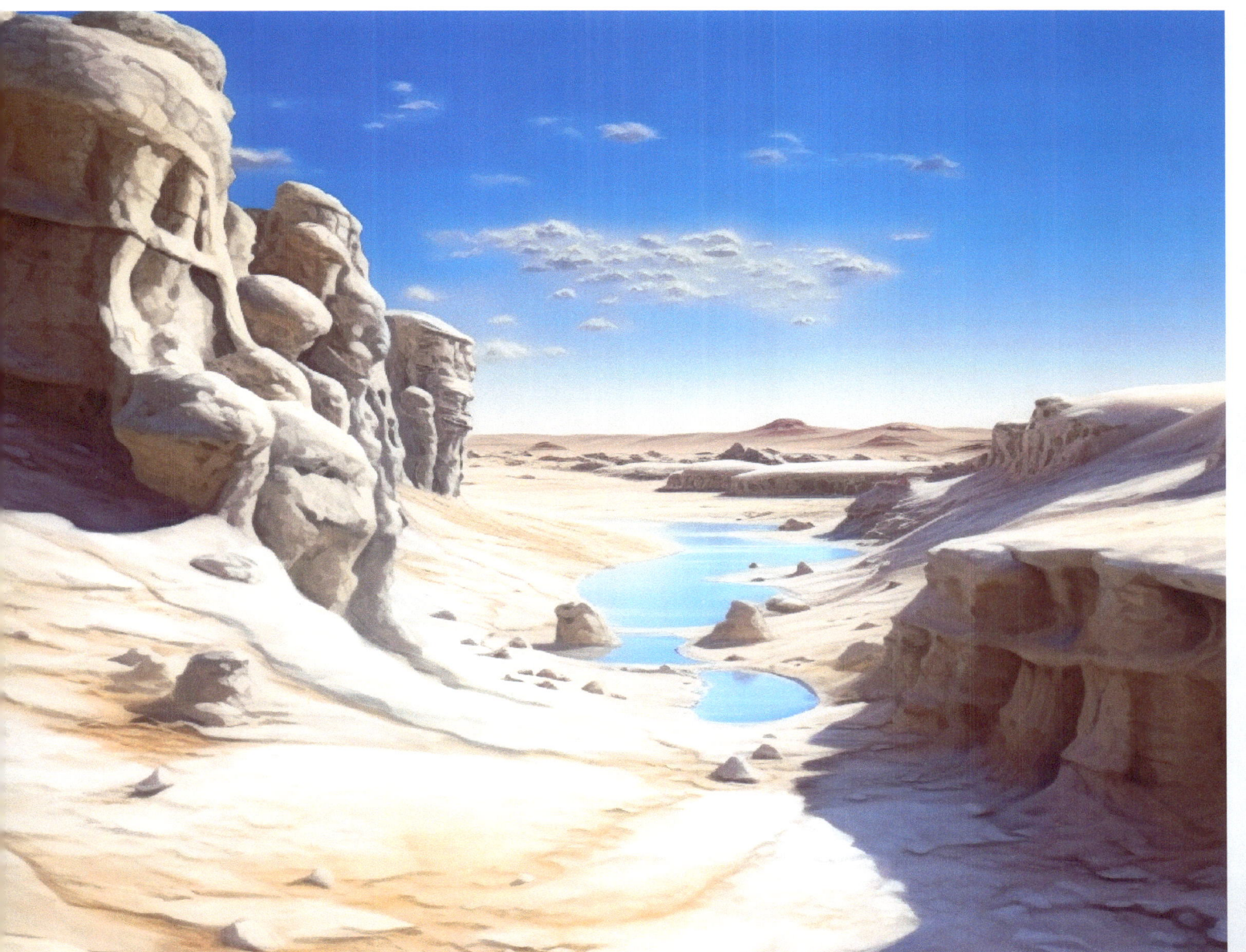

WHITE DESERT

Known for its stunning white chalk formations.

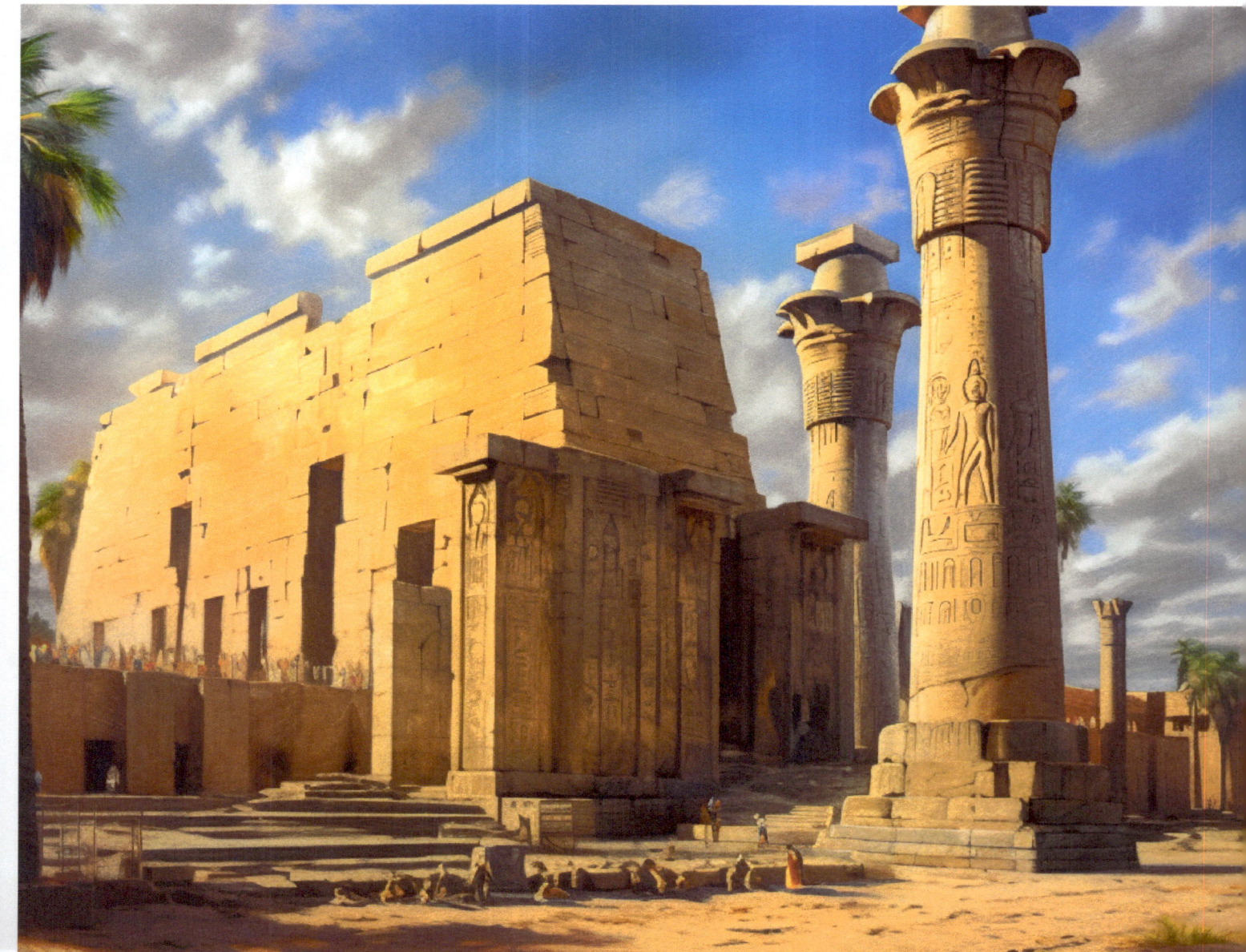

LUXOR TEMPLE

A large ancient Egyptian temple complex.

www.ingramcontent.com/pod-product-compliance
Lightning Source LLC
Chambersburg PA
CBHW041525280526
45792CB00004B/1386